To Arvin

The Lord is your Shepherd

Your friend and neighbor,

Jim Shelley

TWENTY-THREE

New Reflections on the 23rd Psalm and You

By Bishop Jim Swilley

Scripture references and Part One 23rd Psalm are taken from the **New King James Version**. Copyright © 1979, 1980, 1982, 1992 by Thomas Nelson, Inc. Used by permission. All rights reserved. [The author has emphasized some words in Scripture that are not emphasized in the original Bible versions, and all references may not be an exact quote of the referenced verse.]

Part Two: 23rd Psalm taken from **The Message**. Copyright © by Eugene H. Peterson 1993, 1994, 1995, 1996, 2000, 2001, 2002. Used by permission of NavPress Publishing Group.

Part Three: 23rd Psalm taken from the Holy Bible, **Today's New International Version**®. TNIV®. Copyright © 2002, 2004 by International Bible Society. All rights reserved throughout the world. Used by permission of Zondervan.

Part Four: 23rd Psalm taken from **The Bible, A New Translation (James Moffatt)**. New York: Harper & Row Publishers, 1954.

Part Five: 23rd Psalm taken from **THE AMPLIFIED BIBLE**, Old Testament copyright © 1965, 1987 by the Zondervan Corporation. The Amplified New Testament copyright © 1958, 1987 by The Lockman Foundation. Used by permission.

Part Six: 23rd Psalm taken from **The Jerusalem Bible**, copyright © 1966, 1967 and 1968 by Darton, Longman & Todd, Ltd. and Doubleday, a division of Bantam Doubleday Dell Publishing Group, Inc. Reprinted by permission.

Part Seven: 23rd Psalm taken from **New Life Version**, © Christian Literature International.

Part Eight: 23rd Psalm taken from **The Psalms for Today**: A New Translation from the Hebrew into Current English (R. K. Harrison). Zondervan Publishing House.

Part Nine: 23rd Psalm taken from **The New English Bible**, copyright © The Delegates of the Oxford University Press and The Syndics of the Cambridge University Press 1961, 1970.

Part Ten: 23rd Psalm taken from **The Living Bible**, copyright © 1971. Used by permission of Tyndale House Publishers, Wheaton, IL 60189, USA. All rights reserved.

Twenty-Three New Reflections on the 23rd Psalm and You

ISBN 0-9716838-6-7
Copyright © 2006 by Jim Earl Swilley
Published by Church In The Now Publishing
1877 Iris Drive, SE
Conyers, GA 30013
Cover art by Jim Earl Swilley / Cover design by Current Event Productions

Printed in the United States of America. All rights reserved under International Copyright Law. Contents and/or cover may not be reproduced in whole or in part in any form without the express written consent of the Publisher.

TABLE OF CONTENTS

Foreword 11

FIRST WORDS
- ➤ Hearing with New Ears 13
- ➤ Rethinking David's Timeless Masterpiece...........14
- ➤ A Song for You..15

PART ONE: A Time of Transition 19

The Lord Is My Shepherd; I Shall Not Want

1. Your Whole Life Is a Journey........................... 20
2. Your Path Is Unfolding Day by Day. 21
3. You Must Not Fear the Unknown 22
4. You Must Keep Your Eyes Open 23
5. You Must Keep Your Ears Open 24
6. You Must Accept Change 25
7. You Must Keep Moving 26
8. You Will Reach Your Destination 27
9. You Will Not Lack Anything You Need 28
10. Your Future Is in God's Hands 29

PART TWO: A Time of Stillness 31

He Makes Me to Lie Down in Green Pastures
He Leads Me Beside the Still Waters

1. You Are in the Right Place 32
2. You Can Rest Now... 33
3. You Can Let Go Now 34
4. You Have His Peace... 35
5. You Don't Have to Worry 36
6. You Don't Have to Please Everybody............. 37
7. You Don't Have to Have All the Answers........ 38
8. You Don't Have to Fix Everything 39
9. You Must Stay in the Moment........................ 40
10. You Can Be Still and Know That He Is God 41

PART THREE: A Time of Restoration 43

He Restores My Soul

1. You Have the Mind of Christ 44
2. Your Brokenness Is Being Healed 45
3. Your Vision Is Being Restored 46
4. You Don't Have to Have Unnecessary Stress ... 47
5. You Don't Have to Live Under Pressure 48
6. You Can Control Your Thoughts 49
7. You Can Think a New Way 50
8. Your Soul Is Prospering 51
9. Your Latter Will Be Greater Than Your Former ... 52
10. You Are Being Made Whole 53

PART FOUR: A Time of Decision 55

He Leads Me in the Paths of Righteousness for His Name's Sake

1. You Can Make the Right Choice 56
2. You Can Do the Right Thing 57
3. You Can Find the Right Path 58
4. You Aren't Going to Fail 59
5. You Don't Have To Be Afraid of Falling 60
6. You Can Get Back Up Again 61
7. You Don't Have to Second-Guess Yourself 62
8. You Know More Than You Think You Know 63
9. You Must Stay Focused 64
10. You Can Learn from Your Mistakes 65

PART FIVE: A Time of Deliverance 67

Yea, Though I Walk Through the Valley of the Shadow of Death, I Will Fear No Evil, for You Are with Me

1. You Are Not Alone 68
2. You're Going to Get Through This 69
3. You're Stronger Than You Think You Are 70
4. You Must Keep it All in Perspective 71
5. You Don't Have To Be Intimidated 72
6. You Have Nothing to Fear 73
7. You Can't Quit Now 74
8. You Must Keep a Positive Attitude 75
9. Your Second Wind Is Coming 76
10. You Will Live and Not Die 77

PART SIX: A Time of Conflict 79

Your Rod and Your Staff, They Comfort Me

1. You Are Being Protected 80
2. You Have On the Whole Armor of God 81
3. You Have God On Your Side 82
4. You Have the Holy Spirit 83
5. You Have the Word 84
6. You Have Angels Around You 85
7. You Are More Than a Conqueror 86
8. You Will Prevail 87
9. You Are an Overcomer 88
10. You Are Safe 89

PART SEVEN: A Time of Vindication 91

You Prepare a Table Before Me in the Presence of My Enemies

1. You Don't Have to Fear Anyone 92
2. You Don't Need to Get Revenge 93
3. You Don't Have to Prove Your Point 94
4. You Don't Need To Be Ashamed 95
5. You Must Make Peace with Your Past 96
6. Your Enemies Don't Need To Be Destroyed 97
7. You Can Let Yesterday Go 98
8. You Can Forgive Others Now. 99
9. You Can Forgive Yourself Now 100
10. You Can Live Your Life in the Now 102

PART EIGHT: A Time of Prosperity 103

You Anoint My Head with Oil; My Cup Runs Over

1. You Have an Anointing 104
2. You Have Help 105
3. You Have Abundant Life 106
4. You Are Blessed 107
5. You Will Increase 108
6. You Can Be in the Flow 109
7. You Are Going to Prosper 110
8. You Are Going to Succeed 111
9. You're Not Going to Lose Everything 112
10. You Will Have More Than Enough 113

PART NINE: A Time of Progress............................115

Surely Goodness and Mercy Shall Follow Me All the Days of My Life

1. Your Life Has a Purpose............................ 116
2. You Have the Grace of God 117
3. You Have the Mercy of God 118
4. You Have the Favor of God 119
5. You Have the Forgiveness of God 120
6. You Can Be Happy...................................... 121
7. You Can Enjoy Your Life............................. 122
8. You Are Making Progress 123
9. Your Path Is Growing Brighter 124
10. You Can Fulfill Your Destiny 125

PART TEN: A Time of Fulfillment 127

I Will Dwell in the House of the Lord Forever

1. You Are in the Family of God...................... 128
2. You Are Welcome in the House of God 129
3. You Can Be at Peace Anywhere 130
4. You Can Love Yourself 131
5. You Have the Nature of God 132
6. You Can Know the Will of God 133
7. You Don't Have to Envy Anyone 134
8. You Can Have a Fulfilling Life...................... 135
9. You Are in the Presence of God 136
10. You Are Home 137

FOREWORD

The words of the 23rd Psalm are so familiar to most Christians, yet many have never gleaned the full impact of the words penned and sung by the shepherd psalmist. In this great, topical devotional, Bishop Jim Earl Swilley has taken the words and revelation of the psalmist and presented them in such a way that you feel like you are hearing them for the very first time.

Bishop Swilley has taken words that are ancient and made them as fresh as the morning dew. In his own unique way he has made the 23rd Psalm both profoundly relevant and full of amazing revelation. The words of this devotional book become a masterpiece of daily encouragement and life principles that propel the reader to excel in life and soar in the Spirit.

The author divides the text into ten topics, each of which powerfully demonstrates grace for daily living. He will walk you through the transitions of life and into the stillness of rest. You will encounter restoration and decisive victories. Deliverance is manifest as we confront the areas of our life that cause us to live in the past.

These twenty-three principles bring vindication and prosperity. Bishop Swilley clearly gives a vision for a season of progress and fulfillment that is dawning in your life just over the next horizon. In my personal favorite section, he declares that you must make peace with your past. It is impossible to move to the future while still stuck in your yesterday.

I so wholeheartedly endorse both this book and the author. You will be encouraged, edified and uplifted with nothing but the good news. Bishop Swilley is a breath of fresh air in the religious climate of pretentiousness and egotism. He uses his own down-to-earth humor and life experience to make the Word of God come alive. His written words, like his preached sermons, will be life and health to you as you grow in the Kingdom of God.

May you read this devotional and share it with all of your friends. I believe you will walk by the still waters and linger in the green pastures as daily you find restoration for your soul. This is a book for every passionate believer who desires to truly know The Shepherd.

I pray that this book will cause each of us to get a renewed, inspired passion for spending time in the presence of the true Shepherd and may that time produce a true reformation in the Body of Christ. Let it begin today as you read this treatise from the 23rd Psalm.

>Bishop David Huskins, Th.D., D.D.
>Pastor, Cedar Lake Christian Center
>Presiding Bishop, International Communion of Charismatic Churches

FIRST WORDS

Hearing with New Ears

"I pledge allegiance to the flag," "To be or not to be," "We have nothing to fear but fear itself," "I have a dream." These and other similar phrases are instantly recognizable to us, having become so much a part of our collective consciousness through their continuous repetition over the years. Most of our famous speeches or well-known literary passages contain such a phrase – usually an opening line – that serves as a sort of touchstone which enables the hearer to tap into whatever knowledge or understanding they may have of the particular speech or passage. You may not be able to recall any of the content of Lincoln's Gettysburg Address, but as soon as you hear the line, *"Fourscore and seven years ago,"* you become aware that you possess a general sense of association that allows you to relate to the speech and its historic significance. It happens because of the immediate familiarity of those unique and iconic first words.

Amazingly, just the sound of certain familiar phrases can evoke emotional, even visceral, responses from within us. For example, as a child, you most likely could experience a sense of happiness and well-being by simply hearing a parent or teacher speak the phrase, *"Once upon a time."* Those four words automatically activated a positive emotion in you that was connected with the joyous anticipation of being told a wonderful story, even before you actually heard the story. In a similar way, as an adult, you may sometimes inadvertently start laughing as soon as someone merely says to you, *"Have you heard the one about . . .?"* The laugh begins *before* you hear the joke (which may or may not be funny to you) simply because your brain has been conditioned to respond with laughter to the kind of words that generally follow that question.

On the other hand, the words, *"We regret to inform you,"* or *"You'd better sit down for this,"* can instantly darken your spirit and create anxiety in your mind even before you hear any bad news that may follow. As a matter of fact, sometimes the actual bad news isn't as hard on you as is the line or phrase that tries to *prepare* you for the bad news. The dread or negative anticipation that comes from automatically responding to certain familiar words like these can be devastating. Words are powerful and their effect on us is immediate, as well as long-term. And the words or phrases that are the most familiar to us can create feelings, both positive and negative, that influence our lives more than our minds can comprehend.

Rethinking David's Masterpiece

Some of the most universally familiar words in the English lexicon are *"The Lord is my Shepherd, I shall not want,"* the opening lyrics to the psalmist David's best known song and highest artistic achievement. The simple, yet well-crafted lines of Psalm 23 are arguably the ones most frequently cited from the Christian Bible, rivaled only, perhaps, by St. Matthew's account of "The Lord's Prayer" from the King James Version. Even those who have no connection to the Judeo-Christian paradigm or working knowledge of the Scriptures would find these words easily recognizable and even quotable. Like the opening lines to the Gettysburg Address, *"The Lord is my Shepherd"* instantly identifies the larger text.

But there is a certain derived comfort that comes from hearing or reading the 23rd Psalm, not because of its content, but because of the sheer familiarity of it that can prevent the reader or hearer from experiencing the full benefits of the piece. The impact of the message gets lost in the immediate-felt response when the words are recited. As soon as *"The Lord is my Shepherd"* is said aloud in church or at a commencement ceremony, Bar Mitzvah or funeral, it exudes a sense of recognition that causes instant emotional association in the same way as does the phrase, *"Merry Christmas!"* We enjoy hearing the Christmas greeting mostly because our brain associates it with positive feelings that we have developed toward the holidays throughout our lifetime, but the words are basically meaningless to us.

The purpose of this book is to help you hear – *really* hear – David's timeless masterpiece once again and to cause you to love it because of what it says, not just because you know it so well. When we don't really comprehend the words that are most familiar to us, it is like not being able to see the forest for the trees. We easily take for granted what we know (or think we know), and when we hear a commonly known phrase like *"The Lord is my Shepherd,"* we can be immediately comforted by it and sort of "check out" at the same time. We do not discern the meaning even when the words are coming from our own lips. It has been said that people don't know what they like, they like what they know, and, for the most part, that is probably true. But as you read and use this devotional, I pray that you will fall in love anew with the *meaning* of these words and hear them like you've never heard them before.

A Song for You

David, the brilliantly anointed and passionate composer of the Psalms, was creative, complex, conflicted and full of contradictions. He was a warrior, an artist, a deliverer, a musician, a leader, a worshipper, a shepherd, a king, and a very flawed human being. His recorded words display an amazingly wide range of expressed feelings, from the highest emotional highs to the deepest emotional depths. If he were here today, his extreme mood swings would probably be diagnosed as the effects of manic-depression, but he would be able to sit down and talk to you, empathize with everything that you have gone through or are currently experiencing, and then play you an original song about it that would penetrate the deepest part of your soul and bring you peace in your spirit.

Of course his psalms always ultimately glorify God, but they also reflect his feelings about the events of his very full and colorful life. If he lived in society today, the full details of his life story might actually be shocking to some (adultery, murder, scandal, dysfunctional family, etc.), but they enabled him to write songs and poetry that we can all relate to – songs about victory and defeat, love and rejection, betrayal and forgiveness, revenge and peacemaking, sin and repentance, divine worship and human emotion, and everything that all real people experience at some time on some level.

The greatest of these songs is the one that provides the basis for this book. Somehow, this *"man after God's own heart"* was able to speak to the human condition (with all of its glory and pathos) perfectly and concisely in what we now know as the six verses comprising the 23rd Psalm. It is a song about transition and destiny and faith and making peace with your life as you make peace with God. The words on these pages will extract meaning for your everyday concerns from David's beautiful lyrics and expound on them for your own personal meditation. It is a topical devotional rather than one with entries for each day of the year and, hopefully, will help you hear *"The Lord is my Shepherd"* and the rest of the passage like you're hearing it for the first time. May you feel David's spirit as his words locate where you are on your journey in the 21st century and help you reach the place where you can *"dwell in the house of the Lord forever."*

Jim Swilley

TWENTY-THREE

New Reflections on the 23rd Psalm and You

PART ONE: A Time of Transition
The Lord is My Shepherd; I Shall Not Want

> The Lord is my shepherd; I shall not want.
> He makes me to lie down in green pastures;
> He leads me beside the still waters.
>
> He restores my soul; He leads me in the paths of righteousness for His name's sake.
>
> Yea, though I walk through the valley of the shadow of death, I will fear no evil;
> For you are with me;
> Your rod and your staff, they comfort me.
>
> You prepare a table before me in the presence of my enemies; You anoint my head with oil;
> My cup runs over.
>
> Surely goodness and mercy shall follow me all the days of my life; And I will dwell in the house of the Lord forever.
>
> Psalm 23 – New King James Version

1.
Your Whole Life Is a Journey

Never doubt the importance of your existence in the world. You are definitely here on this planet for a reason and the life that you are here to lead is meant to be a meaningful one. Your birth may have been a surprise to your parents, but it was not a surprise to God: **Before I formed you in the womb, I knew you.** The day you were born you automatically took the first step on your life-journey and you have been traveling ever since, which is why you need a shepherd that you can follow and trust to lead you in the right direction to your ultimate destination. God knew that you would be here now: **"just as He chose us in Him before the foundation of the world, that we should be holy and without blame before Him in love,"** and He wants to lead you in your own appropriate paths of righteousness for His name's sake. The Kingdom of God and the world will suffer if you don't successfully complete your journey.

Two streams feed the river of your life. One stream is what many refer to as the *perfect* or optimum will of God for your life, and the other stream is your reaction and response to that perfect will or plan. In the same way that the texture of woven fabric consists of the warp and woof (the woof threads run crosswise at right angles to the warp threads), so the tapestry of your life is being woven by God *and* you. The Lord, your Shepherd, is leading you through your life only because you choose to follow Him, so you are actually co-creating your destiny *with* Him. You can't follow if He doesn't lead, but He can't lead if you don't follow: **"that you may prove what is that good and acceptable and PERFECT will of God."** Following God throughout the entirety of your life-journey is a lifestyle choice. **For as many as are led by the Spirit of God, they are the sons of God.** You'll be traveling for quite awhile, so you might as well enjoy the trip.

2.
Your Path Is Unfolding Day by Day

Rejoice that you have lived to see another day! *Every* day is important. *Every* day matters. The events of each 24-hour period are significant, because a person's whole life can change in just one day. Your path is unfolding day by day and what happens *today* can make a radical difference in your life and in your future. **This is the DAY that the Lord has made.** This very day is a major piece of the puzzle that reveals the big picture even if it seems like any other ordinary day. The Lord is your Shepherd today – right now. He ordained this day for you long before you were ever born and He is available to lead you through it, minute by minute and second by second. Because He loves you, He has provided all the mercy you will need to get through this day. **Through the Lord's mercies we are not consumed, because His compassions fail not. They are new EVERY MORNING.**

Speak well of this day! **For he who would love life and see good DAYS, let him refrain his tongue from evil, and his lips from speaking deceit.** You are not aimless today. You are not without a plan. A morning prayer helps to align your words with the words of the Shepherd concerning the blueprint for this day so that both of you will be on the same page of the plan-book. The day is saying something to you. **DAY unto DAY utters speech, and night unto night reveals knowledge.** Can you hear what the day is saying to you? Listen for today's message so that you can stay on the Shepherd's path. Seize the day! Embrace all that it has to offer, even the difficult parts of it. Don't waste the precious opportunities that it affords you by allowing yourself to view it in a negative light. Don't give in to the temptation to complain about what you think the day lacks. This is *your* path. This is *your* day!

3.
You Must Not Fear the Unknown

Do not worry about tomorrow, for tomorrow will worry about its own things. Sufficient for the day is its own trouble. The Shepherd will always challenge the sheep's comfort zone. He will not let you stay in one place until you starve to death. He must keep you continually moving in order to lead you to green pastures. If you stay in one place you will eat up all of the available food, so you must keep following the Shepherd even when you don't feel like it and even when you have no idea where He is leading you. You must remain mobile at all times and trust that He will always take care of you, even when you are completely exhausted from following His constant movement. ***I know the plans I have for you, says the Lord.*** Remember that even though you are determining most of what happens in your life, you have chosen to follow the Shepherd's leading so, ultimately, you have to put Him in charge of the journey.

What *you* call *the unknown* is not unknown to God at all. The eternal I AM can see what is ahead on the road of your life, and He isn't worried about anything that He sees there. **Trust in the Lord with all of your heart, and do not lean to your own understanding. In all of your ways acknowledge Him, and He will direct your paths.** He will direct you on all the paths of your destiny, both known and unknown, tried and untried. Even when you are pushed to pioneer a primeval forest, He will **make a road in the wilderness.** The Lord is your Shepherd, so you don't ever need to fear the unknown because the unknown is nonexistent to Him. And you must trust that the Shepherd will never lead you into a dangerous place without providing full protection for you. He knows what lies ahead and He knows that He is more than **able to do exceedingly abundantly above all that we ask or think.**

4.
You Must Keep Your Eyes Open

Watch and pray. Jesus gave this admonition to his disciples, exhorting them to be aware of what was around them and of the situation that was about to unfold before them, so they could pray with insight. **Watch and pray.** The admonition is as relevant and necessary today as it was then. Prayer without watching is as ineffective as watching is without prayer. Awareness is not just important, it is *essential*. The shepherd walks ahead of the sheep where he can easily be seen, because sheep have to follow a leader. Cattle are *driven,* but sheep must be *led,* and you must make the effort to keep your Leader in your vision at all times so that you can move when He moves. Continue to remove all visual obstructions in the external world, as well as in your internal universe, so that you may remain totally vigilant – visually connected to the Lord, your Shepherd. **Blessed are the pure in heart, for they shall SEE God.**

In any given day there are a thousand things competing for your attention, trying to get you to fix your gaze on them. You may find yourself overwhelmed by all the things that you have to see to in a day. Sometimes your plate can get so full that you don't want to look at *anything* anymore. You just want it all to go away and, because you know that nothing in your too-busy life is probably going to go away anytime soon, you sometimes just shut down and enter a state of denial where you don't have to look at the path ahead of you or anything that lies on it. But denial is intentional blindness and it never produces anything positive or worthwhile. If you have been walking through life with your eyes closed, it's time to heal yourself from your own blindness and start following the Shepherd again. Open your eyes and courageously look ahead with anticipation, regardless of how you feel. As God said to Moses, **"Look and live!"**

5.
You Must Keep Your Ears Open

My sheep know My voice. If you are going to follow the Shepherd for a lifetime, you must know His voice and know how and where to listen for it. You must learn to listen to your heart. You must be able to listen to the still, small voice within your spirit. You must develop the sensitivity to listen to your own dreams and visions. You must remain open to hearing the confirmation that you receive from the mouth of two or three witnesses. You must listen to God speak through the anointed preaching that you hear, through the songs of worship that inspire you, through the words of the children in your life, and through the miracle of nature and the universe around you. The Shepherd is speaking to you now, and the more you hear Him, the easier it will become to instantly recognize His voice. The more you hear Him, the more centered and grounded you will become (even during transition) and the less confusion you will have to endure.

Faith comes by hearing, and hearing by the word of God. Faith always comes when you hear God speak and, to be able to live the life of faith, you must be able to hear Him speak continually in some form or another. If faith can *come* it can *go*, which is why it must come by *hearing,* not by *having heard*. When you start hearing God regularly, you will become aware that He is also hearing you, and *that* realization will ultimately cause your prayer life to become an ongoing, two-way conversation where you can literally **pray without ceasing.** This level of prayer-communication will cause you to know a dimension of confidence that you have not known before. **This is the confidence that we have in Him, that, if we ask anything according to His will HE HEARS US. And if we know that HE HEARS US, whatever we ask, we know that we have the petitions that we desired of Him.** Keep your ears open today.

6.
You Must Accept Change

If the Lord really is your Shepherd, you must be willing to remain in a constant state of preparedness for seasons of change. **To every thing there is a season, and a time for every purpose under heaven.** The shepherd must lead his sheep *all* year long: in the dead of winter, in the early spring, in the heat of summer, in the cool days of fall. And the sheep must follow, regardless of the weather or the changing temperatures or the conditions around them. The Lord *is* your Shepherd, so don't resist transition. Transition is a necessary part of your growth and development. The Lord *is* your shepherd, so don't think of change as something negative or as something to be feared or dreaded. Change is good. It comes with the territory, so it must be accepted. The Lord *is* your Shepherd, so be flexible and adaptable – always willing to be mobile – always traveling light – always open to His leading.

All living things change constantly and your life-journey is a living thing. There are bends in the road of your life – rough and rocky places, steep hills and deep valleys. The path before you is ever twisting and turning; it has dark places and crooked places. The road is rarely smooth. Sometimes the terrain is hostile and full of dangerous beasts that seek to devour you, but the fearless Shepherd sets His face like an arrowhead and never turns back. He always moves you onward, forward. He knows you can make it, because He knows you better than you know yourself. He sees that the greatness in you can only be revealed through the process of change, so you must not only accept that *things* are changing, but you must recognize that *you* are changing. **We all, with open face beholding as in a glass the glory of the Lord, are CHANGED into the same image from glory to glory, even as by the Spirit of the Lord.**

7.
You Must Keep Moving

In Him we live and MOVE and have our being. For those who follow the Shepherd with their whole heart, transition is not a temporal thing – it's a life-theme. It's not optional, either; it's the Master's mandate for navigation of the paths of righteousness. Movement is a fact of your life in God: ***in Him we MOVE.*** The life that exists in the Spirit experiences a successive changing of place, a constant motion, a daily transit into full conformity to His image. The passage is purposeful and progressive. **The steps of a good man are ordered by the Lord, and He delights in his way.** The Shepherd *delights* in keeping you in step so that you will be sure to finish your course. He stirs you up so that He can complete the evolution of the effect of His word in your life. Your mental mobility and flux of faith are a part of this process and are in total keeping with His plan and will for your life.

Don't be concerned about your feelings of restlessness and don't try to fight or suppress them. They are evidence that the Shepherd is prodding and goading you until you move up to higher ground. **As an eagle stirs up its nest, hovers over its young, spreading out its wings, taking them up, carrying them on its wings,** so the Word of the Lord acts as an irritant to make you leave the nest and learn how to fly on your own. Don't confuse your restlessness with unhappiness. The sheep that knows it is cared for is happily content in transition, and contentment is important **(godliness with contentment is great gain)**, but contentment is not complacency. The Shepherd's rod and His staff *do* comfort you, but they are not designed to make you so comfortable that you decide to stop moving. Find your happiness in the motion. **He who is of a merry heart has a continual feast,** and a continual feast is a movable feast.

8.
You Will Reach Your Destination

You're going to make it. Whatever setbacks you may have experienced cannot keep you from reaching your destination. Don't let the obstacles that you face daily become exaggerated in your mind; your problems are not an indication of the end of the world. The Shepherd has not abandoned you and He is still leading you. If somehow you do happen to lose your way, He will gladly leave ninety-nine others to go find you, no matter how far off you have wandered, no matter what kind of mess you may have gotten yourself into. Your Shepherd is your Savior and He will always rescue you. You will be *safe* because you will be *saved:* **I am the good shepherd. The good shepherd gives His life for the sheep.** Because His mercy endures forever, He will lovingly put you back on the right path because *He* wants you to make it more than *you* want to make it. He has faith in your destiny.

The Shepherd fully intends to finish what He started in you – **being fully confident of this very thing, that He who has begun a good work in you will complete it until the day of Jesus Christ.** The Alpha is also the Omega, the Beginning is also the End, the Author of your faith is also the Finisher of it, and the First is also the Last. **He is also able to save to the uttermost those who come to God through Him, since He always lives to make intercession for them.** He knows how to intercede for you perfectly because He knows you so very well. He knows your strengths and your weaknesses, your virtues and your flaws. **I am the good shepherd; and I know my sheep, and am known by My own. As the Father knows Me, even so I know the Father; and I lay down My life for the sheep.** He knows you the best and still loves you the most. That's why you can know for sure that you're going to make it!

9.
You Will Not Lack Anything You Need

The Lord is my Shepherd, I SHALL NOT WANT. Remember that no matter where He leads you – no matter how long the season of uncertainty – you will never want for or lack anything that you need. You will not go hungry nor suffer any deprivation. **My God shall supply all your need according to His riches in glory by Christ Jesus.** He knows you and He knows what you need even before you ask. Seek first the Shepherd's Kingdom and He will bring you into a place of evergreen abundance. He will never lead you into a dead, dry pasture where there is no provision. **Do not fear, little flock, for it is your Father's good pleasure to give you the Kingdom.** You can pray the Kingdom prayer: **Give us this day our daily bread,** and be fully confident that, even though manna only comes in daily portions, you can always rely on it being there, even for forty years in the wilderness.

The same God who sent ravens to feed a prophet and placed tax money in the mouth of a slimy fish can still show amazing innovation in providing for your needs. The Creator is as creative as He ever was, and as you follow His path you will find yourself flowing in His creativity for your own life. Never worry about lack: **I have been young, and now am old; Yet I have not seen the righteous forsaken, nor his descendants begging bread.** Never worry about your family or loved ones being destitute or going without. Never be envious of what others have; there's enough prosperity to go around. Your Shepherd looks well to the state of His flocks and He is watching over your situation. God is good and He is good to you and your household. He keeps His covenant of goodness to a thousand generations. **The young lions do lack and suffer hunger; But those who seek the Lord SHALL NOT LACK any good thing.**

10.
Your Future Is in God's Hands

The Shepherd, the Lord of Tomorrow, sees and declares the end from the beginning. He blesses you now as an indication of good and even greater things to come to you in time. As you learn the fine points and nuances of following Him daily, you will go from glory to glory, from faith to faith, until you can honestly say that your latter is greater than your former. You have everything to look forward to because you have the assurance that your path, as good as it is now, will actually grow brighter in your future. **The path of the just is like the shining sun that shines ever brighter unto the perfect day.** The Lord is your Shepherd, so you can believe that the best is yet to come for you. That hope is something that you can hold on to when times are hard: **For our light affliction, which is but for a moment, is working for us a far more exceeding and eternal weight of glory.**

Live in the now, but keep your eye of faith on the horizon. **Do not become sluggish, but imitate those who through faith and patience inherit the promise.** There is a beautiful promise over your life. No one is born on the earth without promise and you will receive yours through a lifestyle that has mastered the art of balancing and harmonizing faith and patience. Thank God for yesterday, but let it go. Enjoy today, but look forward to tomorrow with great anticipation. An attitude of expectancy creates an environment for the miraculous. Keep following the Shepherd and hold on to His promise for the future: **Because he has set his love upon Me, therefore I will deliver him; I will set him on high, because he has known my name. He shall call upon Me, and I will answer him; I will be with him in trouble; I will deliver him and honor him. With long life I will satisfy him, and show him My salvation.**

TWENTY-THREE

Part One Notes / A Time of Transition

PART TWO: A Time of Stillness

He Makes Me to Lie Down in Green Pastures, He Leads Me Beside the Still Waters

> God, my shepherd! I don't need a thing.
>
> You have bedded me down in lush meadows;
> You find me quiet pools to drink from.
>
> True to your word, you let me catch my breath
> And send me in the right direction.
>
> Even when the way goes through Death Valley,
> I'm not afraid when you walk at my side.
> Your trusty shepherd's crook makes me feel secure.
>
> You serve me a six-course dinner right in front of my
> enemies. You revive my drooping head;
> my cup brims with blessing.
>
> Your beauty and love chase after me every day
> of my life. I'm back home in the house of God
> for the rest of my life.
>
> Psalm 23 – The Message

1.
You Are in the Right Place

Stop second-guessing and/or over-analyzing your current place in life. Your steps are ordered by the Lord, and if your heart's true desire is to be in His will, then you're just going to have to believe that you're exactly where He wants you to be at this time, even if everything in your life seems to be at a standstill. This is especially true if you have sincerely prayed *in faith* about your destiny. **A double-minded man is unstable in all of his ways.** The same Shepherd who gives marching orders also tells you when to halt, so you must trust Him and refuse to complain when things in your life are not progressing as fast you would like. Even if they are not progressing at all, or seem to be actually going in reverse, you must have faith when you pray about where you *are*, not just about where you are *going*. When it's time to walk, you must **walk by faith and not by sight,** but when it's time to stop walking, you must then *stand still* by that same faith.

Lying down in a green pasture may be the last thing you want to do right now, and you may have no desire whatsoever to be led beside any still body of water, but that might be exactly what is currently on the Shepherd's agenda for you, so you may as well embrace this quiet season and enjoy it for what it is. Besides, there could be more happening behind the scenes than you can realize at the moment, and it's possible that you need some downtime to get yourself prepared for something big that's coming. It's possible to know in your spirit that you are in the right place, even if you have no idea intellectually why you are there. **The spirit of a man is the lamp of the Lord, searching all the inner depths of his heart.** The *inner depths* are the hidden rooms of your spirit and whatever room you now find yourself in is where you are supposed to be. **Having done all to stand, stand;** just stand in the *right place!*

2.
You Can Rest Now

REST in the Lord, and wait patiently for Him. You have been constantly on the move – taking on too much responsibility, burning the candle at both ends – but now it's time to be still. You must rest in your spirit, soul, and body, and that is why the Shepherd is making you lie down in green pastures whether you like it or not. He is *making* you lie down right here where you are – *making* you get quiet and still in spite of yourself – *making* you admit that you have to trust in Him completely concerning the things that are simply beyond your control. It is not an option and you have no choice: **The Lord is in His holy temple. Let all the earth keep silence before Him.** What you thought was a dead-end on your life-path may actually be a green pasture in disguise, a temporary stopping place where you can recharge and be refreshed and renewed before getting back on the road.

In returning and REST you shall be saved; in quietness and confidence shall be your strength. You don't have to say anything right now. You don't have to explain yourself. You don't have to work so hard. Rest is the important thing – the main thing. Don't be anxious about the time that you're potentially going to waste while resting and the possibility of losing ground. This little period of inactivity beside the still waters may be the best thing that could happen to you right now and God can easily restore the time to you, if necessary. Time is never a problem with Him. When the Shepherd starts pushing you to begin moving again, you won't have any difficulty getting caught up. Just move when He says to move and you will be able to make up for anything that has been lost. **There remains therefore a REST for the people of God . . . let us therefore be diligent to enter that REST.**

3.
You Can Let Go Now

Two words to remember while being still: *No regrets!* Whatever has happened *has happened* and you can't change it, so stop wasting your valuable time wondering about what might have been or where you would be now had you done things differently. You can't alter the reality that you did whatever you did (or didn't do whatever you didn't do), so own the responsibility of your choices and actions and move on. The time beside the still waters should be used to re-evaluate and rethink your situation in life and to let go of some things: **one thing I do, forgetting those things which are behind.** The Shepherd didn't call you aside so that you could spend more time punishing yourself for your faults or failures. This should be a season of healing and you can't get better by holding on to negative things from the past. His mercy endures forever, but He can't continue the process of forgiveness until *you* decide to forgive yourself.

You can let go of your disappointments now and still learn from your mistakes so that you don't repeat them. You can let go of your grudges and offenses to others and still expect to be celebrated and treated fairly in the world. You can let go of your need to blame someone (including yourself) for what you think is wrong with your life and still be able to honestly lay the axe to the root of your problems. You can let go of any unrealistic expectations that you may have had for your future and still walk in faith and have a dream. The point is that it's time to unload some of the unnecessary excess baggage that you have been carrying around **(let us lay aside every weight)**, so that you can emerge from this season of stillness happy, light and free. Open up those hands that have been so tightly clutching the past and lift them up in praise to God for His goodness and for the new season that you are ready to face.

4.
You Have His Peace

Silence your mind and meditate on the words that have been written indelibly on your heart by the Spirit of God. In the secret stillness of your own spirit you can move beyond the borders of your thoughts into a dimension where you can communicate with the Shepherd face to face, where you can actually know the mind of God. He is leading you to a quiet place where His peace alone will sustain you. He calms the waves of your emotions by simply saying, **"Peace! Be still!"** and sends a hush over every memory that tries to haunt you: **PEACE I leave with you, My PEACE I give you; not as the world gives do I give to you. Let not your heart be troubled, neither let it be afraid.** Let your soul settle down into a tranquil state where you simply *cannot* fret or have any anxiety about anything. You have the keys of the Kingdom at your disposal, and the Kingdom is **righteousness, PEACE, and joy in the Holy Ghost.**

Illogical peace – a peace that transcends all comprehension – peace that triumphs over the intellect – this is the peace that is available to you. **The PEACE of God, which surpasses all understanding, will guard your hearts and minds through Christ Jesus.** Do not let your heart be distressed or agitated; it isn't necessary. Stop allowing yourself to be disturbed; the peace that you have enables you to rise above any and all circumstances that interrupt your serenity. Do not permit yourself to be fearful; the God-peace that you possess makes you internally invincible. Refuse to let the people in your life push your emotional buttons and get to you so easily. You can settle down and relax now. Think on good things. . . how beautifully green the pasture is and how incredibly still the water. **You will keep him in perfect PEACE, whose mind is stayed on You, because he trusts in You.**

5.
You Don't Have to Worry

Go ahead – exhale deeply and let all the stress and uneasiness that has been trying to attach itself to your mind just melt off you. It's time to regain your composure and move away from the place where you are bombarded with tormenting thoughts. Do not be disquieted, God is with you. **Be careful for nothing; but in every thing by prayer and supplication with thanksgiving let your requests be made known to God.** Do not worry about anything and stop being so easily annoyed and irritated so much of the time. Be anxious for nothing. Let go of all the vexation and distress. It is not God's will that you walk around with a heavy heart and a troubled mind. You were not designed to be discontented. God is giving you peace of mind. God will take care of you. God is for you. God is on your side. God will protect you. God is in control. God is good. God will make everything work out for the best and for *your* good.

Everything is going to be all right. You don't have to lie awake all night tonight. You can sleep soundly without tossing and turning. You don't have to wake up depressed and dreading your day. You don't have to go through your day distracted or in a funk. You can focus on your work and do a good job. You can eat something delicious and enjoy it. You don't have to sit in a strain. You can let your shoulders relax now. Your neck doesn't have to feel so stiff and tight. Your stomach doesn't have to be in knots and your digestion can be normal. You can stop visualizing the worst. You can lighten up and be positive. You can be optimistic and stop taking everything so seriously. You can throw back your head and laugh from your belly. You can look forward to your future. **Therefore I say to you, "DO NOT WORRY ABOUT YOUR LIFE . . . DO NOT WORRY ABOUT TOMORROW, for tomorrow will worry about its own things."**

6.
You Don't Have to Please Everybody

There is no point in wearing yourself out in an effort to make everybody that you know happy with everything about you and with everything that you do. Trying to please everyone involved with your life is about as doable as is flying to the moon – technically it *can* be done, but you know that you're never going to be able to pull it off (unless you're an astronaut and they reopen the lunar space program and you get chosen to be a part of it). No matter how hard you try or how well you perform, somebody somewhere isn't going to be pleased with you. The point is, you just *can't* please everybody – *ever* – and, more importantly, you're not *supposed* to please everybody. If you really know who you are and you believe in yourself, you will not have an unbalanced need for acceptance and approval from others and you can then enjoy healthy relationships that don't just wear you out and frustrate you.

The Shepherd may have brought you aside to make you lie down in this pasture so that you could get away from the influence of opinionated people who want to tell you how to run your life. Remember that the Lord is your *only* shepherd; no one else is qualified to lead you, so your top priority (really your *only* priority) should be to please Him. **Enoch . . . had this testimony, that he PLEASED God . . . But without faith it is impossible to PLEASE Him.** You need to be led beside the still waters so that you can hear His voice again without all the distraction that comes from the voices of others. When you have too much advice – too much input into your head even from well-meaning people – you simply can't hear the Shepherd's voice clearly. Walk in love with everyone, be a servant to others as Jesus taught, be humble and teachable, but don't let anybody run your life but God and you.

7.
You Don't Have to Have All the Answers

It's okay to say, "I don't know." Nobody but God is supposed to know everything and nobody should be expected to: **for we know in part, and we prophesy in part.** Walking by faith as you follow the Shepherd involves constantly dealing with the unknown and the unseen. **Faith is the evidence of things not seen,** and that usually means taking the journey of life one step at a time. It means trusting in the Shepherd to lead you even when you have no idea where tomorrow's provision is going to come from or how He is going to get it to you (or get you to it), and you can't explain to anyone how you know that everything is going to be fine, but you just know that you know, even though you don't know the next step to take. **By faith Abraham obeyed when he was called to go out to the place which he would receive as an inheritance. And he went out, NOT KNOWING WHERE HE WAS GOING.**

If you knew everything, no one could have a relationship with you because you wouldn't need anyone and everyone you know would be intimidated by your omniscience. **Knowledge puffs up, but love edifies.** If you were all-knowing, you would lead a very lonely life, but the good news is that you *don't* know it all. You don't have to figure out everything or solve all the mysteries of the universe. You can be your wonderfully human and limited self and still do amazing things with the help of God and the people He has placed in your life that know things that you don't. Just follow the Shepherd from where you are right now and don't worry about the missing pieces to the puzzle because, at the end of the day, all that really matters is that you know Him: **for I know whom I have believed and am persuaded that He is able to keep what I have committed to Him until that day.**

8.
You Don't Have to Fix Everything

Here's a reality check: life isn't supposed to be perfect, so stop acting like you think that it is. You live in an imperfect world that was intentionally created to be that way. Your relationships aren't perfect. No relationship is perfect because it isn't supposed to be. Your parents weren't perfect, just like their parents before them weren't perfect. Your marriage isn't perfect. When two imperfect people wed, they inevitably create an imperfect union; there's no getting around it. Your kids aren't perfect because they are made from the imperfect DNA of their imperfect parents. Your house isn't perfect; it's built with imperfect materials made from the imperfect earth. You job isn't perfect. Your city, town or neighborhood isn't perfect. Your church isn't perfect and nobody there, including the pastor, is perfect. If there were a perfect church, you could not join it because of your own imperfection. Only God is perfect.

Two things to remember: (1) *There is a God;* (2) *You are not Him*. You are not responsible for all of creation. You did not take away the sin of the world, so you don't have to function as if you were the Head of the Church. You did not die on the cross; there are no stripes on your back or nail scars in your hands or feet. You don't have to be personally offended when others sin because their sin did not cost you anything – you did not pay for it as He did. You do not **ever live to make intercession;** no one will ever stand before your judgment seat, and you will never hand out rewards in eternity. You are free to mind your own business – **work out your own salvation with fear and trembling** – and let Jesus do what only He can and should do. You are not the Holy Spirit; you cannot convict anyone of their sin, no matter how much you hate what they do, so you might as well let God be God and focus on doing *your* best, enjoying *your* imperfect life!

9.
You Must Stay in the Moment

Now is all that matters and nothing is more important than this moment. When the Shepherd makes you lie down in green pastures, it may only be for an instant, so invest yourself in the present so that you can always be where He is. Listen to what God is saying right now. Look at what God is doing in the immediate realm. God is the *I AM* and He dwells only in the eternal *now*. Don't be distracted by the past or the future. Be thankful for what you have in your hand. **Be anxious for nothing, but in everything by prayer and supplication, with thanksgiving, let your requests be made known to God.** Don't worry that it may appear as if all the miracles have already been passed out to others and it's already the eleventh hour. The Shepherd knows what you need and He knows where you are. **Let us not grow weary while doing good, for in due season we shall reap if we do not lose heart.**

Give God your praise *before* you receive the manifestation that you seek. Rejoice while you are still lying down, immovable, in the pasture to which He has led you for this time. Your attitude will make or break you, so keep yours good and current and fresh, free from doubt and unbelief. Stop sabotaging yourself with regret over the past or fear of the future. You're exactly where you need to be right now, so really *be* in the moment mentally and emotionally. Forgive whoever is entangling you internally with yesterday and holding you back spiritually. Whatever has happened is just a memory now, so let it go. That was then. This is now. No addiction to a past offense or grudge is worth you missing what this moment has to offer you. And no unfounded fear about tomorrow is worth your attention. The thing you seek is within your reach – it's been here all along, you just haven't seen it because of your perception. This is your moment – *seize it!*

10.
You Can Be Still and Know That He Is God

The Shepherd has led you to this place for a reason. You have been brought here for this season so that you can know Him like you have never known Him before. **BE STILL, and know that I am God; I will be exalted among the nations, I will be exalted in the earth.** You can only put your full attention on God when you are being completely still, standing in awe of His greatness and majesty, focusing entirely on Him. **Moses said to the people, "Do not be afraid. STAND STILL and see the salvation of the Lord, which He will accomplish for you today."** God is worthy to be praised and worshipped without any unnecessary distraction. Some things may have been removed from you so that you can fully concentrate on Him. Direct all of your energy toward exalting Him and you will see His glory and His salvation. Worship Him with your entire spirit, soul and body. Trust Him with your whole heart.

Then He arose and rebuked the wind, and said to the sea, "Peace, BE STILL!" And the wind ceased, and there was great calm. When the Shepherd commands everything in your life to come into order, the result is a *great calm.* **Meditate within your heart on your bed and BE STILL.** Here in this green pasture you can clear your head and begin to see things correctly. When you let the stress go, the confusion goes with it and suddenly your spiritual vision improves. Now you can re-evaluate your priorities. Now you can be alone with God and with yourself and be content. Now you can dwell in the secret place of the Most High and just *be.* When the dust settles and the smoke clears, you can get your bearings and find your direction again. Here, beside the still waters, everything becomes clear and you find that you are well, you are centered, and you are whole. Be still and know that He is God!

TWENTY-THREE

Part Two Notes / A Time of Stillness

PART THREE: A Time of Restoration

He Restores My Soul

The Lord is my shepherd, I lack nothing.

He makes me lie down in green pastures,
he leads me beside quiet waters,
He refreshes my soul.

He guides me along the right paths
for his name's sake.

Even though I walk through the darkest valley,
I will fear no evil, for you are with me;
your rod and your staff, they comfort me.

You prepare a table before me in the presence of my
enemies. You anoint my head with oil;
my cup overflows.

Surely your goodness and love will follow me
all the days of my life,
And I will dwell in the house of the Lord forever.

Psalm 23 – Today's New International Version

1.
You Have the Mind of Christ

The Shepherd is bringing restoration to your soul . . . to your mind . . . to your emotions . . . to your memories, in a way that only He can. When God restores, He doesn't just take you back to where you were before, He actually brings you into a greater and higher dimension where you are even better and healthier than you would have been had you not needed the restoration in the first place. The restoration of the soul involves a marked improvement in your attitude. **Let this MIND be in you which was also in Christ Jesus,** but it also has to do with the recovery of your perception, intuition and insight. **He who is spiritual judges all things, yet he himself is rightly judged by no one. For who has known the MIND of the Lord that he may instruct Him? But we have THE MIND OF CHRIST.** You have available to you the wisdom of God Himself, revealed within you through the mind of Christ.

When the Shepherd begins the process of restoring your soul, you will find yourself starting to advance in areas where you have previously been in a state of retreat and regression. Restoration creates internal progress – the supernatural recovery of strength – where His redeeming love is able to repair the areas of your psyche that have been seriously damaged through the battles of life. The revelation of that love, which is completely unconditional, will potentially birth a revival of things like long-forgotten dreams and visions that may have been seemingly dead for some time. A season of true restoration allows you to regain lost emotional territory so that you can renew yourself from the inside, out. **But of Him you are in Christ Jesus, who became for us wisdom from God - and righteousness and sanctification and redemption - that, as it is written, "He who glories, let him glory in the LORD."** The mind of Christ belongs to you.

2.
Your Brokenness Is Being Healed

Hopes that have been hatefully harmed and hurt . . . devastated dreams . . . the disappointments of life . . . the basic wear and tear on self-esteem that comes from rejection and the resulting experience of an injured heart – these things cause a sort of breaking down of the human spirit that is both negative and debilitating. But the Shepherd sees and knows and He leads those who are broken into living, green pastures of restoration. **He heals the BROKENHEARTED and binds up their wounds.** He will pick up the pieces of your shattered self-image and will lovingly mend your heart, delivering inner healing and restored confidence to you at the same time. The Shepherd heals and restores the spirit *and* the soul, and the restoration of your soul will bring a new vitality even to your physical being. **The spirit of a man will sustain him in sickness, but WHO CAN BEAR A BROKEN SPIRIT?**

A merry heart does good, like medicine, but a BROKEN SPIRIT dries the bones. He who causes the desert to bloom like a rose will refresh you and re-create a youthfulness within your inner being that will spring up like an eternal well of joy. **Behold, God is my salvation, I will trust and not be afraid; for YAH, the Lord, is my strength and song; He also has become my salvation. Therefore with joy you will draw water from the wells of salvation.** There is an evergreen and life-affirming tree in the center of the Shepherd's pasture that is watered by that well. **Hope deferred makes the heart sick, but when the desire comes, it is a tree of life.** The tree of life is yours; the Lord is turning your captivity and the desired thing is coming to you. And because the Lord is restoring your soul, you are more than just a survivor – your whole existence is becoming a well-watered garden that will produce fruit all the days of your life.

3.
Your Vision Is Being Restored

The Lord answered me and said: "Write the VISION and make it plain on tablets, that he may run who reads it. For the VISION is yet for an appointed time; But at the end it will speak, and it will not lie. Though it tarries, wait for it; Because it will surely come, it will not tarry." The restoration of your soul includes the recovery of your dreams and visions. Because of the leading of the Shepherd in your life, you can believe in them again. You can hope again. You don't have to be afraid to expect the best any more. You can look forward to the future again. You can be glad to wake up in the morning and start with a fresh vision for your day and not be afraid of being disappointed. You can embrace the concept of available possibilities again. You can face forward and be happy with a genuine sense of expectancy and an awareness of promise. Your vision will be the road map to a better tomorrow.

Where there is no revelation (no prophetic VISION) the people cast off restraint. Your vision gives you the discipline to stay in the path and follow the Shepherd on a day-to-day basis. It inspires and motivates you, but its presence no longer causes you to feel anxious and unsettled when you don't see immediate progress in your life. Because of the maturing process of restoration, you can now exercise your faith in all of the potential of your vision and in the big picture of your dreams and still be able to pace yourself to be led by Him one step at a time. *Wherever* He leads you, you can bring your vision with you on the path – His path for you – and simply enjoy the journey for the sake of just being with Him. When you move, you will move toward the fulfillment of that vision, and when you stay put, you will be happy in knowing that the vision still lives and will still be accomplished in its appropriate time and season.

4.
You Don't Have to Have Unnecessary Stress

A limited amount of daily stress is harmless and can, in fact, be beneficial in helping you to acquire peak performance in your regular routine. But unmanaged and unchecked, it can be dangerous and even deadly. Living with it constantly and at high levels is not the will of God for your life and a very important part of your restoration is the elimination of that kind of soul-damaging stress that can easily be life threatening. **O you afflicted one, tossed with tempest, and not comforted . . . in righteousness you shall be established; you shall be far from oppression, for you shall not fear; and from terror, for it shall not come near you.** Peace of mind, restful sleep, calm emotions, the absence of worry – these things can and should be yours. You don't have to carry the weight of the world on your shoulders **(the government will be upon His shoulder)**, because the Architect of all things is able to do it for you.

Relax! It's *all* good because God is good! His mercy *really* does endure forever and He really does cause all things to work together for your good. Your stress and strain have to go because His burden is easy, His yoke is light, and you can cast all of your care on Him because He cares for you personally. **Rest in the Lord, and wait patiently for Him: Do not fret because of Him who prospers in his way, because of the man who brings wicked schemes to pass. Cease from anger, and forsake wrath; Do not fret - it only causes harm.** The Shepherd is restoring the part of your soul or mind that is able to perceive things without the influence of stress – the rational part that is capable of seeing the world with a proper and balanced perspective. Stress distorts your vision, but the Shepherd restores all. Through Him you can live responsibly but freely, because you can see your path from His vantage point.

5.
You Don't Have to Live Under Pressure

The Shepherd is uniquely anointed to help you live a quality life without the constant presence of undue pressure: ***The Spirit of the Lord God is upon Me, because the Lord has anointed me . . . to comfort all that mourn, to console those who mourn in Zion, to give them beauty for ashes, the oil of joy for mourning, the garment of praise for the spirit of heaviness.*** You were not created to live your life under a spirit or atmosphere of heaviness: ***Now the Lord is the Spirit; and where the Spirit of the Lord is, there is liberty.*** The Shepherd is restoring you to freedom, so be free *indeed* – free in your heart and free in your mind – free from the pressures of life. Dare to live the life of liberty and peace. Dare to trust the Shepherd and to believe that He is fully able to lead you successfully without your having to be under a cloud all the time. You can walk in faith without always feeling like you're living on the edge.

Green pastures. Still waters. A restored soul. Let these things become realities in your life. God is great and greatly to be praised, so you can move into a place of burden-removing worship when you are tempted to succumb to pressure. Be led by the Spirit instead of allowing yourself to make decisions in response to the pressure in your life. Good decisions are rarely, if ever, the result of pressured thinking. Think clearly and soberly. Encourage yourself in the Lord and calm yourself. Walk in the Spirit. Ultimately, you are only accountable to God for the direction of your destiny, so don't allow anyone else to pressure you into giving *them* the lordship over your life. Answer to Him only and go only to Him for answers. Focus only on the good and positive in your life: ***I will meditate on the glorious splendor of Your majesty, and on your wondrous works . . . My mouth shall speak the praise of the Lord.***

6.
You Can Control Your Thoughts

He restores your soul. Your thoughts are being restored. Your imagination is being restored. Your ability to visualize is being restored. All negative and counterproductive mental processes are becoming obsolete because of the restorative powers of the Shepherd who leads you by leading the way that you think: **You will keep him in perfect peace whose mind is STAYED on You, because he trusts in You.** No matter how much hardship you have had to deal with on your path, you're not going to lose your mind or deteriorate into an emotional state where you are vulnerable to thoughts of self-destruction. There is a restful green pasture in your inner world and you have the ability to go there anytime. The one who restores your soul refreshes your mind. **Consider Him who endured such hostility from sinners against Himself, lest you become weary and discouraged in your souls (minds).**

You are capable of good, organized and creative thinking. **The THOUGHTS of the righteous are right, but the counsels of the wicked are deceitful.** You can think right. When you commit to following the Shepherd, regardless of the circumstances around you, your thoughts will come into divine order. **Commit your works to the Lord, and your THOUGHTS will be established.** An established mind is a powerful mind. The more you follow the Shepherd, the more you will begin to think like He thinks, and thinking His thoughts is what will cause real and noticeable transformation in your life. **Do not be conformed to this world, but be transformed by the renewing of your mind.** Because He restores your soul, you have the ability to control your thoughts and to move them in a direction that will bring you peace in your life: **for as he thinks in his heart, so is he.**

7.
You Can Think a New Way

A new paradigm – a new outlook – a new perspective is available to you because the Lord, your Shepherd, restores your soul every day of your life. Now you can think in a whole new way and new and better thoughts will ultimately bring new and better things into your world. **The THOUGHTS of the diligent lead surely to plenty.** You don't have to be confused in your mind and you don't have to adopt someone else's point of view because you constantly find yourself second-guessing your own. You can think for yourself. You can have your own opinions and believe in the validity of them without apology. You can trust your own instincts and have faith in your own faith. People will never value your opinions until you value them yourself, and you will only influence others when you believe in the fruit of your own thinking. He has restored your soul, so you can own your thoughts and be responsible for them.

Change is good and necessary and is an important element in your daily discipline of following the Shepherd. But, if you encounter the demands made by the external changes through which He leads you on your path without changing *internally*, you will become overwhelmed with the journey and will be tempted to retreat and to move in reverse. Inevitably, your world is ever changing and you must continually adapt to its evolution if you are going to realize the potential of your life and destiny. You can never successfully deal with change on the outside until you successfully deal with change on the inside. Renewal begins in the spirit and in the mind. **Be RENEWED in the spirit of your mind.** You can change for the better. You can grow and grow *up* by thinking a new way: **When I was a child . . . I THOUGHT as a child; but when I became a man, I put away childish things.**

8.
Your Soul Is Prospering

Beloved, I pray that you may PROSPER in all things and be in health, JUST AS YOUR SOUL PROSPERS. The process and the journey are revealing what has been in you all along, and you are finding that your prosperity and well-being are internal after all. It's all inside you. Your restored soul is manifesting itself as a prosperous one – one that creates health in your physical body and external prosperity in your circumstances. The process of rebirth and renewal is ongoing. ***If anyone is in Christ, he is a new creation; old things have passed away; behold, all things have become new.*** Through the process of following the Shepherd you are finding that old things – old thoughts, old ideas, old paradigms, old agendas – need to pass away so that you can keep moving on the path. To keep up with the Shepherd every day you have to travel light, which means you have to lay aside the thinking that weighs you down.

Desire alone is not enough to bring you to a higher level of existence. ***The soul of a lazy man desires, and has nothing,*** but a prosperous mentality birthed out of a restored soul can change everything for the better. ***THE SOUL OF THE DILIGENT SHALL BE MADE RICH.*** There is a better way to live and it comes through the prosperity of the soul. ***When wisdom enters your heart, and KNOWLEDGE IS PLEASANT TO YOUR SOUL, discretion will preserve you; understanding will keep you.*** You can think the very thoughts of God and never be destroyed for a lack of knowledge because you understand what are the true riches. ***Better is the poor who walks in his integrity than one who is perverse in his lips, and is a fool. Also IT IS NOT GOOD FOR A SOUL TO BE WITHOUT KNOWLEDGE.*** All along the path, as you follow the Shepherd, He imparts His knowledge to you.

9.
Your Latter Will Be Greater Than Your Former

It's all a process. You've heard it said that *success is a journey, not a destination*, and it's true. It's all about the journey and what you learn through it. **I HAVE LEARNED in whatever state I am, to be content . . . Everywhere and in all things I HAVE LEARNED both to be full and to be hungry, both to abound and suffer need. I can do all things through Christ who strengthens me.** Paul did not receive that truth through *revelation*, but through *process*. The whole concept of going from glory to glory is about an ongoing process – a sort of reincarnation, if you will – where you die on one level to live on another. But on the Shepherd's path you find yourself reborn, not as some other thing, but as a better version of yourself. He created you to be *you* and He is helping you to find your true self revealed in Him. And with every rebirth there is a new level of restoration of the soul.

Job certainly went through a process – a very difficult one, indeed – but at the end of it, He was better off than he was at the beginning. His story is a success story. **The Lord RESTORED Job's losses when he prayed for his friends. Indeed the Lord gave Job twice as much as he had before . . . the Lord blessed the LATTER DAYS of Job MORE THAN HIS BEGINNING.** As you follow the Shepherd throughout your life and He continues to restore your soul, you will not just find yourself enduring the journey, but you will benefit from it to the point that your latter days will be better than and superior to your early days. Your life will get better. You will grow stronger. Your relationship with the Shepherd will grow sweeter. Your story will be a success story, as well, and you will have a happy ending that will glorify Him: **With long life I will satisfy him, and show him My salvation.**

10.
You Are Being Made Whole

Whole. Entire. Complete. Finished. These words should describe your ideal, realized mental and spiritual existence because of the true and total restoration of your soul. When He walked the earth, Jesus said many times, **"Your faith has made you WHOLE."** You should know that you have a sufficient measure of your own faith to bring yourself into a place of restored wholeness now, because today He walks the earth in and through you. Your faith is making you whole, and being made *whole* is superior to just being *healed*. Wholeness and soundness is the gift of God, the result of the tireless work of the Shepherd who enables you to patiently and finally say without qualification or reservation, "The Lord is my Shepherd, I shall not want!" Through faith and patience you will inherit the promise of a restored soul. **Let patience have its perfect work, that you may be perfect and complete, LACKING NOTHING.**

It's all coming back to you because the Shepherd came to seek and to save *that* which was lost in your life: **I will RESTORE to you the years that the swarming locust has eaten... you shall eat in plenty and be satisfied, and praise the name of the Lord your God, Who has dealt wondrously with you; and my people shall never be put to shame.** *Now* you can begin to make some sense of why He led you to the green pasture in the first place and why He made you lie down in it. You are restored – no longer fragmented, scattered and double-minded. *Now* you know what you want and what you should do to get it. *Now* you are calm and settled. *Now*, you are solid, anchored, and unmovable. You are *like a tree planted by the rivers of water*, but you finally understand why He led you by the *still* waters and not by the rushing river. *Now* you no longer question the process or His method and you comprehend why it was all necessary.

TWENTY-THREE

Part Three Notes / A Time of Restoration

PART FOUR: A Time of Decision

He Leads Me in the Paths of Righteousness for His Name's Sake

> The Eternal shepherds me, I lack for nothing.
>
> He makes me lie in meadows green, he leads me to
> refreshing streams, he revives life in me.
>
> He guides me by true paths,
> as he himself is true.
>
> My road may run through a glen of gloom,
> but I fear no harm, for thou art beside me;
> thy club, thy staff – they give me courage.
>
> Thou art my host, spreading a feast for me,
> while my foes have to look on!
>
> Thou hast poured oil upon my head, my cup
> is brimming over; yes, and all through my life
> Goodness and Kindness wait on me,
> the Eternal's guest within his household evermore.
>
> Psalm 23 – The James Moffatt Translation

1.
You Can Make the Right Choice

The Shepherd leads you in the *paths* (plural) of righteousness, not the *path* (singular), for His name's sake, and walking in *paths* is all about choice, about choosing the right path for the right season. The quality of your life is the result of a series of decisions and choices that you have made and the declarations that you have uttered concerning those decisions or choices. **The word is very near you, in your mouth and in your heart, that you may do it. See, I have set before you today life and good, death and evil.** You make choices every day and the habit of making good ones can and should be developed and cultivated as the Shepherd leads you in all your paths of righteousness. He will lead you, but you have the ability to *choose* to follow: **I call heaven and earth as witnesses today against you, that I have set before you life and death, blessing and cursing; therefore CHOOSE LIFE, that both you and your descendants may live.**

The personal satisfaction of knowing that you made the right choice about a situation (even if it was an unpopular one) is a priceless treasure: **Obedience is better than sacrifice.** You will face the challenge of choosing from many possible paths in your lifetime, but the ones to which the Shepherd leads you are always the right ones to take. Every morning when you wake up, you are faced with options concerning your attitude and outlook for the day. Because of the sheer power of a decision, you can literally choose the kind of day you are going to have. And all through that day you have the opportunity to choose your reactions to the events that unfold throughout, and those choices will determine how the events will ultimately play out. Never underestimate the power of a decision. **If it seems evil to you to serve the Lord, CHOOSE for yourselves this day whom you will serve . . . but as for me and my house, we will serve the Lord.**

2.
You Can Do the Right Thing

Always do the right thing, regardless of what anyone else does or doesn't do. You have to play the game by the rules whether anybody else does or not, because at the end of the day you will have to answer only to God for your own life, on your own terms. **To him who knows to DO GOOD and does not do it, to him it is sin.** The Shepherd leads you in the paths of righteousness that are basically paths of goodness – paths that lead you to a revelation of the goodness of God so that *you* are able to do good by that very revelation and not because of dead works or religious discipline or anything that is of the flesh. God's goodness is a spiritual thing and it must be spiritually discerned. **God anointed Jesus of Nazareth with the Holy Spirit and with power, who went about DOING GOOD and healing all who were oppressed by the devil, for God was with Him.**

Righteousness simply means *rightness.* The Shepherd leads you in the *paths of rightness* or on the right path, and that means the path or paths that are right for *you.* And the only way to successfully navigate the paths of rightness is to make the decision that you will always do everything in your power to do the right thing – to walk in integrity, to rise above pettiness and small thinking, to take the high road when you could easily feel justified in being hurtful or vindictive to someone, to turn the other cheek and go the second mile. You can do the right thing because you have the nature of God in you and you have the Fruit of the Spirit, which is the *character* of the Holy Spirit. You have the power to choose to follow the Shepherd and to follow His example. **He is the Rock, His work is perfect; For all His ways are justice, a God of truth and without injustice; RIGHTeous and upRIGHT is He.**

3.
You Can Find the Right Path

The Shepherd leads you in the paths of righteousness, but among all those paths there is a *best* path – a *right* path to take – at certain times and for particular reasons. You have a personal journey that only you can take because you have a unique calling and destiny. This is why you must find the word of the Lord for *you* and for the decisions that *you* must make. **Your word is a lamp to my feet and a light to MY PATH.** When you are searching for the right path to take concerning a situation, isolate all the other voices that have influenced your thinking and seek to locate the Shepherd's voice. There is safety in the multitude of counselors, and in the mouth of two or three witnesses every word is established, but *ultimately* you must hear from *God alone* about your journey. When you seek too much advice and listen to the opinions of too many others, you set yourself up for confusion.

It is very important to **trust in the Lord with all your heart, and lean not unto your own understanding.** Your heart, or your spirit, is generally free from the power of outside influences. It is your *understanding*, or the perceptions of your mind, that has been shaped by the world around you, and that is why you have to make the effort not to "lean" on that understanding, or world-view, in order to make spiritual decisions concerning your destiny. You should strive to have good, mental understanding, but it should not be the basis for your direction. **In all your ways acknowledge Him, and He shall direct your PATHS.** He will direct your many paths by leading you one path at a time, one step at a time, as you acknowledge Him in all your ways – the way you think, the way you make decisions, the way you live your daily life. **As many as are led by the Spirit of God, these are the sons of God.**

4.
You Aren't Going to Fail

You're not going to fail because God will not – *cannot* – fail you! You don't have to endure any fear of failure in your life at all: **My lovingkindness I will not utterly take from him, nor allow my faithfulness to FAIL.** You can absolutely put your confidence in the Shepherd who is forever faithful. **Through the Lord's mercies we are not consumed, because His compassions FAIL NOT. They are new every morning; Great is your faithfulness.** It is irrelevant that you may have failed previously, because your past is not an indicator of your future. That was then, this is now! Besides, the memory of your failure, or *perceived* failure, is more than likely exaggerated in your mind. Most of the people in your life probably don't even consider what you think of as your worst failure to really be that at all. Don't be so hard on yourself. It is possible that you have been more successful than you realize.

Prepare yourself to prevail. David psyched himself to win in battle by rehearsing his past victories: **Moreover, David said, "The Lord, who delivered me from the paw of the lion and from the paw of the bear will deliver me from the hand of this Philistine." And Saul said to David, "Go, and the Lord be with you."** Follow his example and don't allow the fear of failure to prevent you from believing in yourself. Remember how many times you have already made it and encourage yourself with that line of thinking. Go ahead and make a decision with the confidence that you are going to succeed, and see how God blesses it. **You will also declare (decree) a thing, and it will be established for you; So light will shine on your ways.** Light, or insight, is going to shine on your ways so that you can clearly see the path of success before you. The Lord is your Shepherd and He is leading you all the way to the top through paths of righteousness!

TWENTY-THREE

5.
You Don't Have To Be Afraid of Falling

Peter walked on the water, and even though he fell beneath the waves, he still did something that no one else in history ever did, besides Jesus Himself. People who never fall are people who never do anything, and it is much more respectable to be a wet water-walker than a dry boat-dweller. You can't let the fear of a fall paralyze you and keep you clinging to the supposed safety of the boat's interior or prevent you from exploring the full potential of the path that the Shepherd has mapped out for you. The Lord is your safety and your strong tower. He has not given you a spirit of fear and He cannot and will not bless cowardice in any way. You've got to keep moving and you have to move in faith – in the unshakable belief that you will always land on your feet. **He will not allow your foot to be moved; He who keeps you will not slumber.** The One who leads you in the paths of righteousness will always be there for you.

My brothers, be all the more eager to make your calling and election sure. For if you do these things, YOU WILL NEVER FALL. What an amazing promise! The more sure that you are of your personal calling, the less likely it will be that you will *ever* fall! You can follow the Shepherd all the days of your life on a firm footing, knowing that **the righteous will never be uprooted** and that you can stay upright on your path, no matter the weight that is on your shoulders. Regardless of what is going on in your life right now, and in spite of what you think could potentially happen tomorrow, continue to fearlessly walk on your path. You're going to make it, and you're going to be safe and sound, reaching your destination in one completely whole piece. Never fear! **A thousand may FALL at your side, and ten thousand at your right hand, but it will not come near you.**

6.
You Can Get Back Up Again

If for some reason you do happen to fall while traveling on a particular personal path of righteousness, you need to know that your fall is not fatal – it's not the end of the world – and that you can get back up again. **A righteous man may fall seven times and RISE AGAIN, but the wicked shall fall by calamity.** You can actually fall "seven" times (seven is the number representing infinity) and get back up. In other words, for every fall there is a potential resurrection. There is no shame in *falling* down; there is only shame in *staying* down, so, if and when you do fall, the quicker that you get back up, the better. And don't feel sorry for yourself for falling. Self-pity just keeps you down on the ground and even causes you to regress. The Shepherd demands that you pick yourself up, dust yourself off, and get moving again, because He knows that you have a lot of ground to cover before sundown.

And don't pay any real attention to those who are eager to point out to you or rehash all the details of your fall, especially those who want to accuse you because of it. **Do not rejoice over me, my enemy; WHEN I FALL, I WILL ARISE; when I sit in darkness, the Lord will be a light to me.** You have to show them that when you get back up you'll be stronger and better than you ever were before – that you will arise to a whole new level – a higher dimension – not just as a survivor, but as one who is more than a conqueror! You'll even be able to look back on your fall with no regrets and may even be inclined to declare that in the long run it was the best thing that could have happened to you because of the clarity that it brought in your life. You can celebrate the fact that you have resurrection power inherent within you. **ARISE, shine; for your light has come! And the glory of the Lord is risen upon you.**

7.
You Don't Have to Second-Guess Yourself

You should always remain teachable and never forget that there is room for growth and improvement in your life at all times. But at some point on your journey you should acquire enough experienced confidence to know who you are and what you want and to learn how to be true to yourself without doubting your own individual strength. **He who doubts is like a wave of the sea driven and tossed by the wind . . . he is a double-minded man, unstable in all his ways.** The Lord is your shepherd; you shall not lack resolve or be deficient in wisdom. You don't have to hesitate or doubt your cognitive skills, because you have the mind of Christ. And remember that He leads you in the paths of righteousness **for HIS name's sake,** so it matters to Him that you do well on your every path, because the reputation of His name is at stake through your life. If you don't look good, He doesn't look good because you bear His name.

Uncertainty is not healthy and it is not the will of God for your life. The more you second-guess your ability to make godly decisions, the more unstable and unreliable you will become about everything that you think or feel. The just shall *live* by faith and that means that *you can know that you know that you know* what you believe and what you should do, without reservation. As Elijah said to the prophets of Baal, **"How long will you waver between two opinions?"** You must have a clear vision of your path and then move on what you believe is the Shepherd's leading. If you are submissive to Him, He will correct you, if necessary. But if He offers no obvious correction you must assume that you are doing the right thing and then do it with self-assurance. You must refuse to have "two opinions" about your direction. Just move in faith and don't look back. And don't worry, God will take care of you always.

8.
You Know More Than You Think You Know

Let that abide in you which you heard FROM THE BEGINNING. Because you were in God "in the beginning" at creation, before the foundation of the world, you have His eternal knowledge and wisdom buried somewhere deep within you and you know more than you think you know. **The anointing which you have received from Him ABIDES IN YOU, and you do not need that anyone teach you; but as the same anointing teaches you CONCERNING ALL THINGS, and is true, and is not a lie, and just as it has taught you, you will abide in Him.** It is through the process of following the Shepherd throughout your life, and all that is revealed in and to you through both the good and bad, the easy and difficult parts of your journey, that your real, deep knowledge comes to the surface. As you progress in your understanding that the Lord is your Shepherd, your heart will teach your mind.

You have an eternal word resident within you that can lead you through the most challenging times of your life: **Brethren, I write no new commandment to you, but an old commandment which you have had FROM THE BEGINNING. The old commandment is the word which you heard FROM THE BEGINNING.** You don't have to run around all over the place trying to find direction or a word from God. You don't have to seek advice from everybody or stay in a constant state of confusion. You don't have to be unsure of yourself or of your ability to hear the voice of the Shepherd with precision and accuracy. You don't have to wait for a word of prophecy to tell you what to do. Just listen to what you "heard from the beginning" and you will find your answers. The Shepherd is leading you, full circle, back to your future where you can finally walk in what you've known all along.

9.
You Must Stay Focused

It is of the utmost importance that you stay focused right now! Keep your eyes on the Shepherd. Look straight ahead. Listen for His steady voice. Don't allow irrational fears to create a distraction in your mind and get you off-track. Look at how far you've already come and recommit yourself to finishing your course with integrity. Regardless of how you feel at the moment, concentrate on your own purpose and your own mission and on what God is doing with and through you **for such a time as this.** Pay attention to your life and the path that is ahead of you, as well as the goals that you have set for yourself. God is trying to tell you something: **wisdom is crying out in the streets.** The word of the Lord is abundant and accessible: **The word is near you, even in your mouth and in your heart.** Be very aware of what the universe is saying to you: **The heavens are declaring the glory of God.**

Don't waste your time trying to straighten out everyone else on their paths, and don't look to the right or the left of you. Enjoy the undisturbed peace that comes from simply minding your own business and following the plan for your own life. Stay focused in your faith and in your prayer life. Streamline your life as much as is possible, especially if your plate is currently too full. Protect your priorities. Know the difference between what is *vital* and what is simply *important,* and make it your aim to take care of the vital things before you do anything else. Let go of the things in your life that are really just time-wasters and move on from unproductive relationships that aren't going anywhere. The Holy Spirit will help you maintain your focus: **The Lord God will help me; therefore I will not be disgraced; therefore I have set my face like a flint, and I know that I will not be ashamed.**

10.
You Can Learn from Your Mistakes

Everybody makes mistakes. No one is perfect, including you, so you should never expect absolute perfection from yourself. Only God is perfect. You should always try to do your best, but after you know that you have done your best, you must accept the outcome of your efforts – *whatever* it is – and be content with your resulting situation in life. You may have disappointed others or yourself, or worse, you may feel that you have disappointed the Shepherd Himself. But you can't please everybody, no matter how well you do. And you can't allow a mistake to shut down your life. As far as the Shepherd is concerned, through His unconditional love for you He continues to lead you ever forward, regardless of your shortcomings. He doesn't look back and, therefore, expects you to refuse to look back, as well. **Forgetting those things which are behind, and reaching to those things which are ahead, I press toward the goal.**

A big mistake can strike a significant blow to self-esteem and self-confidence. It can cause frustration in your ability to make decisions because of the fear of a repeated error. But you can learn from your blunders and emerge smarter and better informed if you know how to view them correctly. By recognizing your faults and limitations you can prevent yourself from stumbling and making the same false steps in the future. You don't have to be defeated by your mistakes. In fact, you can actually be empowered by them by admitting and owning up to them and by making the effort to be educated by them. **Who can understand his errors? Cleanse me from secret faults. Keep back Your servant also from presumptuous sins; Let them not have dominion over me.** Mistakes are a fact of life, but they don't have to dominate you. When you accept your imperfections and forgive yourself, you will discover that the Shepherd has been leading you all along.

TWENTY-THREE

Part Four Notes / A Time of Decision

PART FIVE: A Time of Deliverance

Yea, Though I Walk Through the Valley of the Shadow of Death, I Will Fear No Evil, for You Are with Me

> The Lord is my Shepherd
> [to feed, guide and shield me]; I shall not lack.
>
> He makes me lie down in [fresh, tender]
> green pastures; He leads me beside the still
> and restful waters.
>
> He refreshes and restores my life (my self);
> He leads me in the paths of righteousness
> [uprightness and right standing with Him – not for
> my earning it, but] for His name's sake.
>
> Yes, though I walk through the [deep,
> sunless] valley of the shadow of death,
> I will fear or dread no evil;
> for You are with me;
> Your rod [to protect] and Your staff [to guide], they
> comfort me.
>
> You prepare a table before me in the presence of my
> enemies. You anoint my head with oil;
> my [brimming] cup runs over.
>
> Surely or only goodness, mercy and unfailing love
> shall follow me all the days of my life,
> and through the length of my days
> the house of the Lord [and His presence]
> shall be my dwelling place.
>
> Psalm 23 – Amplified Bible

TWENTY-THREE

1.
You Are Not Alone

Know that you are not in any way isolated, forgotten, or disconnected right now; the light of God is all around you and His presence is filling any and all empty spaces in your consciousness: **And, lo, I am with you always, even to the end of the age.** God is completely aware of you and your circumstances. You are the center of His attention and He is totally focused on your smallest prayer – listening, caring, anticipating your next words. **Fear not, for I have redeemed you, I have called you by your name, you are mine.** He is here for you, acknowledging your every breath and counting your every heartbeat. Don't be afraid to do what you need to do or to go where you need to go; He is with you every step of the way, guarding and guiding, preparing and protecting you. He is with you because He wants to be with you, and He loves you because He wants to love you.

Be quiet and listen . . . you will hear His voice . . . **Call to me and I will answer you and tell you great and unsearchable things you do not know.** The Lord will go before you and surround you with His love. He is above you and under you and in you and around you. **Surely, goodness and mercy will follow you all the days of your life.** The Lord is good. The Lord is on your side. The Lord is your healer. The Lord is your friend, your companion, your nearest relative and closest kin. You have not been abandoned and you need not fear rejection. You will not be cut off. His love is unconditional and everlasting, so there is no reason to dread being alone tonight or any time in the future – even in old age – because He is with you and in you. God is love and God loves you and He will always, always, always love you. **Nothing can separate you from His love** . . . or His mind . . . or His heart. You are not alone.

2.
You're Going to Get Through This

Through . . . hold on to the meaning of that word because you are, without a doubt, going to come *through* this trial . . . season of sorrow . . . period of pain . . . time of testing, with a story and a happy ending! **Yea, though I walk THROUGH the valley of the shadow of death, I will fear no evil.** The valley is temporal, transitory – a passageway to permanent occupancy in the Lord's house. **Through** . . . a wonderful word that speaks of progressive movement. You're coming *through,* you're going *through,* blessed when you come in, blessed when you go out. **When you pass THROUGH the waters, I will be with you.** The power of the promise lies in the word "*through.*" You will not waste away in the water. The "Water-Walker" will bring you to the other side. **When you pass THROUGH the rivers, they shall not overflow you.** The raging river will not become your runny grave.

Through . . . the word speaks of an ongoing promise. **When you pass THROUGH the fire, you will not be burned, neither shall the flame set you ablaze.** Trial by fire creates intense and strangely familiar heat. You've witnessed the fury of the flames before and you've come full circle *through* the fire in times past. But this time you will not just come *through* without the smell of smoke, you will ultimately **come THROUGH the fire as pure gold. Through** . . . the word evokes a sense of hope – an awareness of a confident and favorable expectation. In Him you live and move and have your being. You will live *through* this. You will move *through* this. You will have all of your being as you come *through* this difficult time with flying colors. You're passing *through,* so resist the temptation to become attached to a foreign land where you are unable to sing Zion's songs. Pass *through* your wilderness until you find your land of promise. Push *through* your pain until you are healed and whole. Press *through* your dark night until your new day dawns!

3.
You're Stronger Than You Think You Are

Even though you are, basically, what you *think*, you actually have hidden reserves of strength that are beyond the borders of your mental attitude. That's good information to have because you know that you can't afford to give in to weakness and fear right now. Too much is at stake and too many people (both in heaven and on earth) are depending on you to make it. You can't wait for strength to come to you later. **Be STRONG in the Lord, and in the power of His might** is an admonition that comes without an option. Everything *external* is declaring it *to* you, as everything *internal* is declaring it *within* you. Don't *try* to be strong – just *be strong*. You can do it because you *have* to do it, and you have to do it *now!* You have to tap into your inner reserve of strength now! Embrace the promises of God now! **In your weakness He is made STRONG** now! **Let the weak say I am STRONG** now!

You are indeed **STRENGTHENED WITH MIGHT by His Spirit in the inner man** even though you may not currently be aware of it in your "outer man." It may be hard to *feel* strength right now. In fact, you may not have felt strong for some time, but that is beside the point, presently, because *now* is all that really matters. You don't have the time or energy to try to sort out the past – even the recent past – in an attempt to understand how things in your world got the way they are. But the good news is that when you simply decide to be strong and face the circumstances in your life, strength actually begins to manifest through the power of that decision. So rejoice in knowing that **the joy of the Lord is your STRENGTH** now! **The Lord is your light and your salvation . . . the Lord is the STRENGTH of your life** now! Say, *"I can do all things through Christ who STRENGTHENS me now!"*

4.
You Must Keep it All in Perspective

It's going to be OK . . . really. **Trust in the Lord with all your heart.** There is great and awesome power within your heart. It is the power to believe and the power to release your faith through trust. God is trustworthy, but you must trust Him with *all* of your heart, not just a piece of it. **Lean not unto your own understanding.** Don't be afraid to trust your own instincts, but don't try to figure it all out, either. You can't rely on your ability to understand, mentally, right now. Strive to comprehend with your spirit and don't bother with all the complexities of the human mind. **In all your ways acknowledge Him, and He shall direct your paths.** He will direct your *paths* (plural). This current path is just one of many on which you will travel in your lifetime and God can be trusted to direct each and every one of them for you. Follow Him one step at a time and this present path will not overwhelm you.

Magnify the Lord with me, and let us exalt His name together. Magnify Him, and your problems will immediately appear to be diminished. The bigger God becomes in your sight, the smaller your challenges will look to you. **When my heart is overwhelmed, lead me to the rock that is higher than I.** Keeping your eyes fixed on that enormous Rock will allow you to maintain perspective on every situation. Regardless of the size of the mountain looming ahead of you on your path, God is just simply bigger. Period. Big worship helps to create big faith. Big worship creates a big vision of a big God with a big plan for your life. **If your eye is healthy, your whole body will be filled with light.** Perspective is all about seeing the right thing and looking at things correctly: **Great is the Lord, and greatly to be praised.** Don't waste today on fear or self-pity – look at God. **God is great, and greatly to be praised.**

5.
You Don't Have To Be Intimidated

Don't be afraid of shadows and smokescreens, and don't let yourself believe a lie. Things are rarely, if ever, as bad as they first appear, so don't overreact to the shadow of death. Don't allow bad news to become exaggerated in your mind. **The righteous will be in everlasting remembrance . . . he will not be afraid of evil tidings.** Refuse to accept and entertain a negative report. If you keep your eyes on the Shepherd you will notice that He is never afraid or intimidated, so follow His example as you follow His leading. **God has not given you a spirit of fear (INTIMIDATION), but of power, and of love, and of a sound mind.** And remember that the one who wrote the lyrics to this song knew something about overcoming intimidation. He learned it early in his life when he ran toward the giant Goliath and killed and dismembered him. **Greater is He who is in you than he who is in the world.**

Your own faith will bring you through your valley, and you have more than enough of it to get results for yourself. **If you have faith as a mustard seed, you can say to this mulberry tree, "Be pulled up by the roots and be planted in the sea," and it would obey you.** Have faith in your faith! Faith is your appropriate lifestyle – **the just shall live by faith** – so believe your way through the dark and shadowy places. **For we walk by faith and not by sight.** You may feel nothing but confusion and uncertainty right now, but put one foot in front of the other anyway. Your faith will give you safe passage. Don't be intimidated by the fear of what could or may happen tomorrow. Cross each bridge when you get to it and you'll find that little by little, one step at a time, you'll get through this dangerous place. **Now faith is the evidence of things not seen, the substance of things hoped for.**

6.
You Have Nothing to Fear

FEAR NOT, for I have redeemed you; I have called you by your name; you are Mine. Remember that you are not just a follower of the Shepherd – you actually *belong* to Him! He has a vested interest in protecting and preserving you, so you can rejoice and relax in the reality that He has redeemed you. This is something that *you can know that you know that you know*. You can say with confidence, **"I know that my Redeemer lives!"** He redeemed you because He loves you, and He loves you because He redeemed you, *and* **there is NO FEAR in love, but perfect love CASTS OUT FEAR.** Remember who you are and Whose you are. You are strong. You are blessed. You are redeemed. You are anointed. You are forgiven. You are whole. You are safe. You are able. You are worthy. You are understood. You are heard. You are loved. You are adopted and accepted, so you might as well be fearless!

Worrying about your current situation or circumstances isn't going to help you one bit and it isn't going to get you anywhere. Absolutely nothing positive or productive can come from worry. At best, it is pointless; it won't solve your problems and is a complete waste of your time. At worst, it can be deadly; it can negatively affect your health in a number of ways and can cause the things that you fear to come upon you. Worry is meditation on the negative. It is an unhealthy preoccupation with the dark side. It is perverted faith – a mutation of your powerful ability to believe. Worry and anxiety are fear's evil twins, and they will always try to lead you in the wrong direction. Never listen to them; don't pay them any attention. The Lord, your Shepherd, is your Caretaker, so trust in Him completely and listen only to His loving voice – **Casting all your care upon Him for He cares for you.**

7.
You Can't Quit Now

If you quit moving forward right now, you could potentially end up living the rest of your life in the valley of the shadow of death. The Shepherd knows when you're tired and want to throw in the towel, and He knows that you may be at the breaking point right this minute. **For we do not have a High Priest who cannot sympathize with our weaknesses.** But you can't quit now. You can't give up . . . not here! Not now! You've come too far and you know too much. Too much has been invested in you. Now is the time to be strong and put what you have learned to the test. Now is the time for your confidence to be at an all-time high. **Do not cast away your confidence, which has great reward. For you have need of endurance, so that after you have done the will of God, you may receive the promise . . . now the just shall live by faith; But if anyone draws back, My soul has no pleasure in him.**

He didn't bring you this far to leave you here, so you know that you must find the strength within yourself to move forward. Encourage yourself in the Lord! Take up your bed and walk! Remember your past victories! Think about what you have to lose if you quit! Stir up the gift that is in you! Stop listening to the people who always bring you a negative report! Refuse to give in to any old defeatist thinking that you know is not relevant to your life anymore! Let faith arise in your heart! Stop being so easily intimidated! Stop feeling sorry for yourself! Stop believing in the worst-case scenario! Stop playing the victim role! Get back up when you fall down! You know deep down in your heart of hearts that you are going to be all right, so get back to where you should be mentally and emotionally and start making some plans for your future right now! Remember that God has never given up on you, so you can never give up on Him!

8.
You Must Keep a Positive Attitude

Finally, brethren, whatever things are true, whatever things are noble, whatever things are just, whatever things are pure, whatever things are lovely, whatever things are of good report . . . regardless of the circumstances, and in spite of how bad things may seem to be on the surface, if you look a little deeper, a little farther, past the immediate, you'll see that there are so many wonderful and beautiful things happening to and for you right now. You must remain focused on those positive aspects of your life . . . ***If there is any virtue and if there is anything praiseworthy - meditate on these things.*** It may initially seem inappropriate and perhaps even impossible to try to count your blessings in your current frame of mind, but the blessings are all around you nonetheless, and if you look for them, they'll be very easy for you to count. If you know where to look, the goodness of God will be obvious.

A positive mental attitude is attractive. Thinking good thoughts on a regular basis draws more good things to your life. **To them that have, more will be given.** If you are going to have a positive mentality, you must *choose* to think positively every day of your life. **Be transformed by the renewing of your mind.** Look for the good. Choose to be happy and proactive. God still looks at His creation and says, **"It is good,"** so you can and should follow suit and look at the life that you have created and call *it* good, because it is the only life that you will ever have. Decide to enjoy your journey and you will discover that there is even good to be found in the valley of the shadow of death. Even though you are moving through it and out of it, you can still find the positive somewhere in the now. Remember that He is with you even in this valley. **You will keep him in perfect peace whose mind is stayed on you.**

9.
Your Second Wind Is Coming

You're not dead yet! Take a deep breath and get in the flow of the Holy Spirit who is always standing by to help you. **God is our refuge and strength, a very present help in trouble.** You have *present* help – help in the now! You have the life of God! **But if the Spirit of Him who raised Jesus from the dead dwells in you, He who raised Christ from the dead will also give life to your mortal bodies through His Spirit who dwells in you.** Your youth is being renewed like the eagle's as you experience a supernatural refreshing – a second wind coming from the depths of your soul and spirit. The Shepherd is leading you through the valley of the shadow of death in this time of deliverance. This is your finest hour. Prayer will make you stronger and stronger: **building yourselves up on your most holy faith, praying in the Holy Spirit.** You are being energized by the very Spirit of God.

He gives power to the weak, and to those who have no might He increases strength; your strength is increasing right now. **Even the youths shall faint and be weary, and the young men shall utterly fall.** The fatigue you feel is not about your age, but a second wind is coming no matter how old you are or how tired you may feel. **But those who wait on the Lord shall renew their strength:** you have the ability to renew your own strength by waiting on God through your praise. **They shall mount up with wings as eagles:** you can spread your wings in worship. **They shall run and not be weary:** the power of God is driving weariness from your mind and heart and body. **They shall walk and not faint:** you have the life-giving, life-sustaining promise of the Spirit. **Not by might, nor by power, but by My Spirit says the Lord of hosts.** Ready or not, your second wind is coming.

10.
You Will Live and Not Die

Yea, though I walk through the valley of the shadow of death, I will fear no evil, for you are with me. This valley is just where death casts its shadow; it is not where you will actually die. Shadows are nothing to be afraid of and this is not the end. In fact, it is only the beginning. Death will not sting you and the grave will not be victorious over you. Life always conquers death. **The law of the Spirit of LIFE in Christ Jesus has made [you] free from the law of sin and death,** and you are more than a conqueror. And the fiery trial that you have been enduring is not going to kill you, either; it is actually making you stronger and sharper and purer. You do not have to fear anything evil on any level. Fear no evil in your relationships. Fear no evil that would wage war on your spirit, soul, or body. Fear no evil report. Fear no evil imagination. Fear no evil from the past, present, or future, for He is always with you.

Death and LIFE are in the power of the tongue. What will you say about your life? More importantly, what does God say about it? ***Thus says the Lord God to these bones: "Surely I will cause breath to enter into you, AND YOU SHALL LIVE."*** God says you will live and not die. What do *you* say? How about repeating the words to this Psalm: ***You are my hiding place; You shall preserve me from trouble; You shall surround me with songs of deliverance.*** Or what about saying these words from the living heart of the Psalmist: ***I shall not die, but LIVE, and declare the works of the Lord.*** What are the words to *your* psalms? What is your unique praise to the Source of your life? The Lord is your Shepherd – you will be delivered – you can rest on the promise of it. ***I have come that they might have LIFE, and that they might have it more abundantly.*** You will live and not die!

TWENTY-THREE

Part Five Notes / A Time of Deliverance

PART SIX: A Time of Conflict

Your Rod and Your Staff, They Comfort Me

> Yahweh is my shepherd, I lack nothing.
>
> In meadows of green grass he lets me lie.
> To the waters of repose he leads me;
> there he revives my soul.
>
> He guides me by paths of virtue
> for the sake of his name.
>
> Though I pass through a gloomy valley,
> I fear no harm;
> beside me your rod and your staff
> are there, to hearten me.
>
> You prepare a table before me under the eyes of my
> enemies; you anoint my head with oil,
> my cup brims over.
>
> Ah, how goodness and kindness pursue me,
> every day of my life;
> my home, the house of Yahweh,
> as long as I live!
>
> Psalm 23 – The Jerusalem Bible

TWENTY-THREE

1.
You Are Being Protected

The Lord, your Shepherd, is fully qualified to successfully maintain the guardianship of your whole life: past, present, and future. He is watching over you at all times. **Have you not known? Have you not heard? The everlasting God, the Lord, the Creator of the ends of the earth neither faints nor is weary.** The One who daily numbers the hairs that grow out of your scalp also cares about every detail that flows out of your existence, and it is His good pleasure to have full custody of every single part of you. You needn't feel overwhelmed by the storms of your life because you are completely surrounded and enveloped by His loving-kindness and tender-mercies. His unshakable stability will anchor you through the hardest of times so that you will not be violently tossed around on the sea of life. You no longer have to be afraid or even feel disoriented. **When my heart is overwhelmed, lead me to the Rock that is higher than I.**

You are in the charge of a loving Father who is also a mighty warrior. **A thousand may fall at your side, and ten thousand at your right hand; but it shall not come near you.** The safekeeping of your internal and external life is of the utmost importance to Him. You are being looked after. You are shielded from harm because He covers you and screens out anything that could potentially destroy you. He will preserve and defend you with a holy barrier that guarantees your immunity from the darkness. He is your champion. You are not out there on your own. You are not isolated or vulnerable. You have not lost your way, even if you think or feel that you have. He knows where you are and where you have been. He has seen your nightmares and He shines a light on everything that goes bump in the night. You are in His hand and no one can pluck you out of it. **No weapon formed against you shall prosper.** He's got you!

2.
You Have On the Whole Armor of God

You're stronger than you think you are, and in the time of conflict you will discover that you possess an undeniable inner strength that flows from the heart of the Shepherd, Himself. You will also find that His rod and staff will comfort you by miraculously translating themselves into your concept of the whole armor of God. **Be strong in the Lord and in the power of His might.** There is a defensive covering over your whole life that is activated simply by your daily decision to be strong in the Lord. **Put on the whole armor of God, that you may be able to stand against the wiles of the devil.** You don't have to be overwhelmed by the negative forces of darkness that work against you. You can stand against them and keep standing. In fact, you must develop and live a lifestyle that demonstrates *standing room only* because you are destined to win. **Having done all to stand, stand.**

Stand therefore, having girded your waist with truth – never be afraid of the truth, because the truth will always set you free. Your right-standing with God will protect your spiritual vital organs at all times – **having put on the breastplate of righteousness** – and when you wear the shoes of a peaceful gospel you will always walk in the right direction – **having shod your feet with the preparation of the gospel of peace.** You can have faith in the fact that your own faith will protect you – **above all taking the shield of faith** – and the confidence to know that your comprehension of salvation and your revelation of the word of God will salvage your mind and your thought-life – **take the helmet of salvation and the sword of the Spirit, which is the word of God.** You actually have on the whole armor of God, Himself! What or whom do you have to fear? You're going to be just fine.

3.
You Have God On Your Side

What then shall we say to these things? If God is for us, who can be against us? Really, there is nothing else that needs to be said. The Lord of all creation is in your corner and, no matter what happens to you, you can be sure that He's got your back. What could be better than that? Even when you are in the wrong, and even in the times when He corrects or rebukes you, you still have the assurance that He is ultimately for you and will always faithfully defend you. Only someone who is on your side could work all things together for your good. Only someone who loves you unconditionally could be that committed to your vindication and protection. Only someone who sees the bigger picture of your life and destiny could look beyond your shortcomings and always be there for you. ***I called on the Lord in distress; the Lord answered me and set me in a broad place. The Lord is on my side; I will not fear. What can man do to me?***

His rod of correction comforts you. It does not cause you any pain but, rather, yields the peaceable fruit of righteousness. ***My son, do not despise the discipline of the Lord, nor be discouraged when you are rebuked by Him; For whom He loves He chastens.*** Privately, in your own prayer closet, He may rebuke you, but publicly He will defend you as a good father would defend His children. He is not objective when He sees you, because your life is interpreted through your position in the Christ Who has been wounded for your transgressions. He is already predisposed to take your part and judge you in righteousness. He chose you before He built the world in which you live, and so He is destined to take your part and be on your side. And because you trust in His boundless love, you do not flinch when He corrects you. ***When I cry out to You, then my enemies will turn back; This I know because God is for me.***

4.
You Have the Holy Spirit

The Shepherd, whose rod and staff are always there to comfort you, has promised you another Helper . . . another Comforter . . . another dimension of Himself. **If you love Me, keep my commandments, And I will pray the Father, and He will give you another Helper, that He may abide with you forever - the Spirit of truth.** You have access to the most intimate of relationships, because He has opened up a realm to you whereby He may dwell eternally within your inner being through the personhood of an abiding Spirit. There is one God **(Hear, O Israel, the Lord your God is one)**, but He is capable of a multifaceted manifestation in your everyday life. The Spirit of God is teaching you all things – reminding you of that which you heard from the beginning. **But the Helper, the Holy Spirit, whom the Father will send in my name, He will teach you all things, and bring to your remembrance all things that I said to you.**

The Shepherd, revealing Himself to you as the Holy Spirit, will lead you out of anything that stifles the truth in your life. He will lead you into all of the truth that there is, even if and when it challenges your comfort zone and destroys your traditional prejudices. **When He, the Spirit of truth has come, He will guide you into all truth; for He will not speak on His own authority, but whatever He hears He will speak; and He will tell you things to come.** And, most importantly, He will lead you from the inside, out. **The Spirit of truth, whom the world cannot receive, because it neither sees Him nor knows Him; but you know Him, for He dwells with you and shall be in you.** God is in you by His Spirit, the same Spirit which raised Jesus from the dead. The Shepherd's rod and staff are a part of your internal workings. His voice is leading and guiding you, helping you, comforting you. You are filled with His Spirit!

5.
You Have the Word

In the beginning was the word, and the word was with God, and the word was God. Everything begins with the word of the Lord, and He is the last word on everything. You, along with all other living things, can trace your origins all the way back to His first utterance of ***"Let there be light!"*** You were birthed out of His word and actually *are* a word from His mouth. Your life exists because there is something that God wants to say through you as a living epistle. You are meant to be a message from God to the world. The purpose of your life – the sum total of all the things that you have experienced – is to ultimately become the word made flesh. That's why His word alone is a lamp to your feet and a light to your path, and that's why you find His rod and His staff so comforting: ***I rejoice at Your word as one who finds great treasure.*** You love the word of the Lord because you are made from it.

You have the ability to hear the Shepherd speak to you through your own voice – ***The word is near you, in your mouth and in your heart*** – and you can have the confidence to believe that His word in your own mouth is completely trustworthy. But He can and will speak to you through other media to confirm to you that in the mouth of two or three witnesses every word is established. ***The entrance of your word gives light; It gives understanding to the simple***. God is speaking, and He is speaking to you . . . in you . . . through you. He holds all things together with the word of His power, and He readily reveals that word to your life every day, line upon line, and precept upon precept. The word that He has spoken over your life will not return to Him void, but it will accomplish something good and important. Your life will not be lived in vain. ***Forever, O Lord, Your word is settled in heaven.***

6.
You Have Angels Around You

The angel of the Lord encamps all around those who fear Him, and delivers them. You have heavenly attendants at your disposal – supernatural messengers of God that are always there for you – no matter how many enemies come up against you. ***Do not fear, for those who are with us are more than those who are with them.*** As Elisha prayed that the eyes of his young servant would be opened so he could see that the mountain was full of horses and chariots of fire, so you must know by the Spirit that you are surrounded by a host of angels to protect you at all times. ***He will give His angels charge over you, to keep you in all your ways.*** As the Shepherd leads you, the angels will keep and protect you in every way that you have to go. And if you hit a snag on the path, they will be there to get you back in the flow, ***they will bear you up in their hands, lest you dash your foot against a stone.***

Angelic protection is a part of your inheritance: ***Are they not all ministering spirits sent forth to minister for those who will inherit salvation?*** Because the Lord is your Shepherd, you are in a constant state of receiving ministry, so you have every reason to believe that every situation will not just work out, but that everything will work out for your good. More importantly, everything will work out for God's ultimate purpose. Your angels are always standing by, waiting for instructions that come from you as you speak God's words: ***Bless the Lord, you His angels, who excel in strength, who do His word, heeding the voice of His word.*** You must give voice to the word of the Lord by speaking it out of your mouth, because it is the language of the angels – it is what they understand. And because they excel in strength, they are an amazing resource for you that no longer needs to go untapped. The Lord is your Shepherd; you shall not lack angels.

7.
You Are More Than a Conqueror

You were born to take dominion: **Let us make man in our image, and let him have dominion.** You were born to take charge. You were born to bring change. You were born to be a champion. The Lord, your Shepherd, sees your life from His unique perspective, within the context of His larger plan, and that is why He is committed to leading you all the days of your life. He is directing you in a much bigger role than you can comprehend – one that plays dramatically into the grand scheme of things. **In all these things we are more than conquerors through Him who loved us.** It is in your make-up – in your very DNA – to win, to triumph, to excel. He who loved you, and continues to love you and will always love you, created you for excellence. Your confidence flows out of your belief that you are truly loved. That sense of dominion must be evident in everything that you do and say.

You were born into the chaos and dysfunction of the world so that you could help to bring positive change to it. Something deep within you aspires to restore order to a chaotic environment. The Shepherd is not just leading you because of you. He is leading you so that you may recover sight to the blind and so that you may live out your life as a repairer of the breach. Being more than a conqueror is about bringing glory to God. **Let your light so shine before men, that they may see your good works and glorify your Father in heaven.** Always remember that you are not being protected by the Shepherd's rod and staff because you are a pathetic victim. On the contrary, you are being protected and watched so closely because of the great investment that He has made in you. You must be guarded because you are so valuable to Him. There was never anyone exactly like you, and there will never be another.

8.
You Will Prevail

Because His rod and staff comfort you and safeguard your life, you can move forward to accomplish the things you want to accomplish: ***I can do all things through Christ who strengthens me.*** This declaration is yours to make because the Shepherd has seen to it that your potential to prevail has no boundaries. You can follow Him every step of the way and still be able to determine in your own mind what you want to do with your life. He is leading you, but He wants you to develop your skills in decision-making. And the most important thing you can do right now is to decide not to fail. He says to you, ***"I set before you life and death, blessing and cursing, therefore, choose life."*** Choose to live and not die. Choose to succeed and to prosper in everything that you do. Choose to manifest your own dreams and fulfill your own prophecies. Choose to make it all the way, as you direct your life forward to the fulfillment of your destiny.

The hand of the diligent makes rich. Be diligent to access His rod and staff whenever and wherever you need them. **The hand of the diligent shall bear rule.** Be diligent to follow the Shepherd into places where you can exercise dominion so that He may be glorified. **The plans of the diligent lead surely to plenty.** Be diligent to consult the Shepherd about all of your plans, and then be even more diligent to execute them. You will prevail over every obstacle, including the restraints of time, to pursue your God-inspired goals. **Do you see a man who is diligent in his business? He will stand before kings, he will not stand before unknown men.** In a little while from now you will be able to see why you have been led to take the path which you have taken. It has been rough at times, but it has not been a mistake or a waste of your time. **Whatever you do, do all to the glory of God.**

9.
You Are an Overcomer

These things I have spoken to you, that in Me you may have peace. In the world you will have tribulation; but be of good cheer, I have overcome the world. Listen to your spirit. There you will hear the voice of the Shepherd speaking things to you right now that will cause you to have peace. His words will put the tribulations of the world in proper perspective so that you may truly be of good cheer. The bottom line is this: if He has overcome the world, you can overcome it, too. Just think of all the things that you have already survived – things you thought would kill you, but that actually served to make you stronger in the long run. Remember the lessons you have learned – most of them from your own mistakes – and then find your confidence in the wisdom that you have acquired. You can face your future without fear. Don't be afraid to confront anything that stands in the way of your progress.

For whatever is born of God overcomes the world. And this is the victory that overcomes the world - our faith. Never underestimate the overcoming force of your own faith. It can move mountains when it is used and applied properly. Your faith alone can win victory after victory. Just believe. Only believe. Never stop believing. With man it is impossible, but not with God. With God, all things are possible. ***I write to you, fathers, because you have known Him Who is from the beginning. I write to you, young men, because you have overcome the wicked one.*** The Lord is your Shepherd. You will not go under. He has made you the head and not the tail, above only and not beneath. It is in you to overcome whatever presents itself to you as an obstacle. The Lord is your Shepherd. Never give up. Never settle for less. Never stop believing in His plan for your life. You are an overcomer!

10.
You Are Safe

The Lord is your Shepherd. The Lord is the Good Shepherd – *your* Good Shepherd. The Lord is good. The Lord is good to you all the days of your life. His mercy endures to reach into the lives of your children's children . . . even unto a thousand generations. He watches over you at all times. He is a Savior, and He will save you to the uttermost through His intercession for you. His name is called Faithful and True for a very good reason. You are free of danger or injury because He has secured your life. He is reliable, and you can be certain that He watches over His word in you to perform it. You have immunity from the forces of evil. **Because you have made the Lord, who is my refuge, even the Most High, your dwelling place, no evil shall befall you, nor shall any plague come near your dwelling.** You are protected . . . sheltered in His arms . . . shielded from danger . . . assured of a good outcome.

I will both lie down in peace, and sleep; For you alone, O Lord, make me dwell in safety. You can sleep soundly, knowing that your faith has ultimately made your life risk-free. He is awake when you are not. And when you do awake to find new mercies every morning, you can rest assured that your God is dependable to make a day for you in which you can rejoice and be glad. And you may go through your whole day unharmed and whole, remaining unhurt, always knowing that no matter what happens, everything ultimately will always be all right for you and yours. The Shepherd wants to show you His goodness all the days of your life. And if you are in the heat of a horrible fiery trial even at this moment, you are still safe. This, too, shall pass. After a great storm comes a great calm, and your time of peace is coming. Relax. **The name of the Lord is a strong tower; the righteous run into it and are safe.**

TWENTY-THREE

Part Six Notes / A Time of Conflict

PART SEVEN: A Time of Vindication

You Prepare a Table Before Me in the Presence of My Enemies

The Lord is my Shepherd.
I will have everything I need.

He lets me rest in fields of green grass.
He leads me beside the quiet waters.

He makes me strong again.
He leads me in the way of living right with Himself
which brings honor to His name.

Yes, even if I walk through the valley of the shadow
of death, I will not be afraid of anything, because
You are with me. You have a walking stick with
which to guide and one with which to help.
These comfort me.

You are making a table of food ready for me
in front of those who hate me.
You have poured oil on my head.
I have everything I need.

For sure, You will give me goodness and
loving-kindness all the days of my life.
Then I will live with You in Your house forever.

Psalm 23 – New Life Version

TWENTY-THREE

1.
You Don't Have to Fear Anyone

The Lord, your Shepherd, is your Champion and Vindicator. You don't have to fear *anyone* because He is faithful . . . faithful to preserve and protect you . . . faithful to prepare a beautiful table for you right in the presence of your enemies. **The Lord is my light and my salvation; Whom shall I fear?** Your fear is futile, your panic is pointless, and your worry is worthless. The Shepherd is looking out for you at all times, so there is no reason for you to be in a state of distress. You are in no way vulnerable to exposure to danger, because He is right where you are at all times. Your expectation of pain can easily be removed by simply remembering who you are and *Whose* you are: **The Lord is the strength of my life; Of whom shall I be afraid?** When you feel the temptation to give in to anxiety, dread, or terror, just cry out to Him and He will deliver you from the horrors that you have imagined.

Your God is a big God, and in the presence of His greatness, your fright and timidity will be dwarfed and dissipated. Don't be alarmed by the empty threats of those who would seek to sabotage your life and destiny. You were not designed to live out your days in trepidation and apprehension. You can relax. You can breathe. You never have to be scared or frightened, nervous or edgy. The Shepherd is calling forth the courageous part of you that refuses to live hesitantly. **The Lord is on my side; I will not fear. What can man do to me?** You have His word, His promise, His oath, and His guarantee that you're going to be all right. Never give anyone else power over your life by allowing them to intimidate you in any way. Be at peace. **When I cry out to You, then my enemies will turn back; This I know, because God is for me.** Be strong. **In God I have put my trust; I will not be afraid. What can man do to me?**

A TIME OF VINDICATION

2.
You Don't Need to Get Revenge

In the big picture, reprisal and retribution are not necessarily satisfying. You should aim higher and trust God to even the score: **Vengeance is Mine.** You have better things to do with your life and your precious time than to sit around plotting your revenge for some suffered wrong, whether real or imaginary. You've got to learn to let a thing go. You may not have been able to see that all-important big picture for quite some time now, simply because you've been so absorbed with looking at what "they" did and what you wish you had done about it or had said to them . . . or what you would like to do to them. **O Lord God, to whom vengeance belongs - O God, to whom vengeance belongs, shine forth!** It's time for you to get things in perspective and stop acting out from the center of your hurt. If you really want revenge, you've probably already given up too much time to the offender in your thought-life.

You've been called to something more important and much greater than merely getting even with someone. **Do not be overcome by evil, but overcome evil with good.** Set your goals by a higher standard and on a grander scale than just pettily desiring the chance to even the score. God and nature and life itself will avenge you in due time and in proper order. You don't need to give a person a taste of their own medicine or to exact retribution from them. Revenge is empty and leaves you feeling hollow and unfulfilled. Revenge is just a bad idea. **Do not rejoice when your enemy falls, and do not let your heart be glad when he stumbles; lest the Lord see it, and it displease Him, and He turn away His wrath from him.** Set yourself free by praying these words: **"Father, forgive them, for they do not know what they do,"** and trust the Shepherd and in His principles of sowing and reaping. God is good; move on.

3.
You Don't Have to Prove Your Point

Some people are just never going to get it. No matter how well you communicate your viewpoint to them, they are never going to be able to see things from your perspective, so you will waste your time and energy in trying to prove your point to them. You should, of course, always try to communicate and express yourself in the best way you can (everybody needs and deserves to be heard), but you must be realistic in your expectations of the effect of your communication. **Whoever will not receive you nor hear your words, when you depart from that house or city, shake the dust from your feet.** You have something valid to say and you should say it, but also remember that **there is a time to speak and a time to be silent.** The appropriate time to speak must be discerned, but the time to be silent is always when you realize that your words are inevitably going to fall on deaf ears.

You have absolute assurance that the Shepherd is always going to prepare a table before you in the presence of your enemies, even the harmless and seemingly friendly ones, so, at the end of the day, does it really matter that you were proved right? God knows what is right and He knows your heart; ultimately, that's what is most important. You have His unconditional understanding, and that's really all you need and should be all that you want. Besides, the truth finds its own way to surface and survive, even without your help, so build your confidence on trusting in the truth for all things. It has been said that there are three sides to every story: (1) your side, (2) the other person's side, and (3) the truth. Always seek for the truth in every situation, because the truth is more important than self-preservation or self-defense. And always remember, **we have an Advocate with the Father, Jesus Christ the righteous.**

4.
You Don't Need To Be Ashamed

The Lord, your Shepherd, bore all of the shame of your entire life in His own body in the atonement. You never need to be embarrassed by anything that has caused shame in any part of your personal history; you never have to be hesitant or reluctant to live your whole life without intimidation. **You shall not be ashamed or disgraced forever and ever.** If you are conscience-stricken or remorseful about anything you have done, or anything that has been done to you, only allow yourself to feel that way in an effort to take personal responsibility and ownership of your own actions. **Then you will know that I am the Lord, for they shall not be ashamed who wait for Me.** Jesus was humiliated in your stead when He was crucified, naked, on the cross. You don't have to be sorry. Hold your head high, knowing that you are forgiven because He bore your shame. Be proud of His finished work, and live your life boldly.

Do not fear, for you will not be ashamed; Neither be disgraced, for you will not be put to shame; For you will forget the shame of your youth. You don't have to regret anything that has happened throughout your entire life. Whatever happened, it was what it was and God is greater than anything that you have experienced, no matter how negative or embarrassing. Where your sin has abounded, His grace has much more abounded. **He has not dealt with us according to our sins, nor punished us according to our iniquities.** The Lord, your Shepherd, is proud to prepare a table for you, even in the presence of the enemies (the internal enemies) that you yourself have created. He knows you better than you know yourself and He still loves you, unconditionally. Come to the table with confidence and look right in the face of your enemies while you eat the feast that He has laid out before you.

5.
You Must Make Peace with Your Past

The Lord is your Shepherd: you shall not lack resolution to your life-issues. The Lord is your Shepherd: you shall not want for closure. He makes you lie down temporarily in green pastures and then He urges you to move on. **Brethren, I do not count myself to have apprehended; but one thing I do, forgetting those things which are behind and reaching forward to those things which are ahead, I press toward the goal for the prize of the upward call of God in Christ Jesus.** He leads you beside the still waters where you can accept whatever has happened to you, without condoning whatever shouldn't have happened. He restores your soul so that you can forgive yourself. He leads you in the paths of righteousness so that you can learn from your mistakes. Even though you walk through the valley of the shadow of death, you are empowered to fearlessly face your future without the burden of an unresolved past.

Jesus said to him, "No one, having put his hand to the plow, and looking back, is fit for the Kingdom of God." He prepares a table for you in the presence of your past, and it is there that He anoints your head with the oil of gladness that frees you to live in the now. Your cup of understanding runs over. You can make peace with your past because goodness and mercy follow you all the days of your life, and you dwell in the house of the Lord – not in your past, but in your concept of forever. The house of the Lord is not haunted by the ghosts of the past. The house of the Lord is a household of peace. **Leaving the discussion of the elementary principles of Christ, let us go on to maturity.** It's time to put away childish things and make peace with your past – every part of it – no regrets, no looking back, no second-guessing anything, no driving in reverse. **Remember Lot's wife.**

6.
Your Enemies Don't Need To Be Destroyed

The Lord, your Shepherd, prepares a table for you in the presence of your enemies for many reasons. He wants to see you walk in the overcoming power of love and forgiveness. He wants you to find your inner strength by boldly facing the ones you fear. He wants to show you off as He vindicates you and works all things together for your good. He wants you to live in total freedom from intimidation. **I say to you, love your enemies, bless those who curse you, do good to those who hate you, and pray for those who spitefully use you and persecute you.** Your enemies – even the ones who are actively hostile and antagonistic toward you – are actually helping you to become the *best you* that you can be. Your adversaries are serving to define you and strengthen you. When you learn to respond to them correctly, even your worst foes will actually turn out to be blessings in your life in the big picture.

Whether you realize it or not, your enemies have probably been instrumental in helping you get to where you are today. On some level, you already instinctively know that they are playing an important role in your life, in the same way that Joseph's brothers helped him to become the Pharaoh of Egypt through their horrible actions toward him. Whatever has been done to you, rise above it. Love wins. **I say to you who hear: "Love your enemies, do good to those who hate you, bless those who curse you, and pray for those who spitefully use you. To him who strikes you on one cheek, offer the other also."** At some point your enemies may need to be scattered, but they do not need to be destroyed. **Love your enemies, do good, and lend, hoping for nothing in return; and your reward will be great, and you will be sons of the Most High. For He is kind to the unthankful and evil.**

7.
You Can Let Yesterday Go

You can let go now. The sun has set on the former things, and a new day has begun. Yesterday might as well be a thousand years ago as far as God is concerned. **For a thousand years in Your sight are like yesterday when it is past.** You can stop holding on to the familiar comfort of your bitterness and regret. All that is old news . . . yesterday's headlines . . . obsolete information. It's time to embrace the morning light and prepare your heart for tomorrow's promise. Whatever is over is over – don't live in denial – accept it, fearlessly and graciously. Look ahead, but live your life in the now. **Beloved, do not forget this one thing, that with the Lord one day is as a thousand years, and a thousand years as one day.** The Lord, your Shepherd, prepares a table before you with today's manna, presented on a fresh tablecloth with clean dishes. There are no leftovers served at His banquet. Everything is new.

Holding on to yesterday prevents you from connecting with the miracles of today. Move on in faith, even if the memories of past events are breaking your heart. Your heart will heal in time, and the sooner you replace the comma with a period at the end of the sentence, the sooner you can write your next chapter, or even a whole new wonderful story. **Do not remember the former things, nor consider the things of old. Behold, I will do a new thing, now it shall spring forth; Shall you not know it?** It may be time to rethink everything, even the people (including the enemies) in your life. The Lord is preparing a breakfast table before you in the presence of your enemies, where His mercies are new, as they are every morning. **Behold the former things have come to pass, and new things I declare; Before they spring forth I tell you of them.** There is a new door opened before you – it's time to walk through it.

8.
You Can Forgive Others Now

Nothing in the world of human relationships is more empowering than forgiveness. **Blessed are the merciful, for they shall obtain mercy.** The Lord, your Shepherd, prepares a table of vindication for you, and you can enjoy all the benefits of that table because you know in your heart that you are greater than intolerance. Give yourself permission to embrace the "seventy times seven" principle, because the practice of it will connect you with the limitlessness of the universe (seven is the number of infinity). The blueprint of the Kingdom is laid out in the prayer that Jesus taught His disciples: **Forgive us our trespasses, as we forgive those who trespass against us . . . Forgive us our debts, as we forgive our debtors.** It's time to put away the grudges . . . the offenses . . . the bitterness, and fill yourself to the full at the clean table of the Lord. All is forgiven at His table, and everyone who partakes of it is restored.

When you forgive others, they no longer have power over you. **Whenever you stand praying, if you have anything against anyone, forgive him that your Father in heaven may also forgive you your trespasses.** Forgiveness puts people and things in perspective. It clears your vision so that you can plainly see the path ahead of you. When you forgive, you restore yourself to proper mental and emotional health. And in the grand scheme of things, forgiveness makes you more productive and, ultimately, more successful. **Judge not, and you shall not be judged. Condemn not, and you shall not be condemned. Forgive, and you will be forgiven.** The Lord, your Shepherd, prepares a table for you in the presence of those who need to be forgiven by you, and when you do forgive them you will find much more enjoyment in the meal that He has prepared for you and them. Forgive them. It's what He wants you to do.

9.
You Can Forgive Yourself Now

Confess your trespasses to one another, and pray for one another that you may be healed. The effectual, fervent prayer of a righteous man avails much. It's OK to be imperfect. The effectual, fervent prayer of a *righteous* man (not a *perfect* man) avails much. He has made you righteous by His free gift of justification to you. Righteousness is something that you *are*, not something that you *do*. ***Elijah was a man with a nature like ours, and he prayed earnestly that it would not rain; and it did not rain on the land for three years and six months.*** You should, of course, produce righteous works, while remembering at all times that *you* are not *your behavior*. You are in Christ and it is His righteousness that is motivating your life. Keep your eyes on the Shepherd and set yourself free from your unrealistic self-expectations. Always try to do your best, and forgive yourself when you don't.

Neither do I condemn you. Liberate your own heart by deeply receiving His mercy that endures forever. He has forgiven you, so you must come into agreement with Him by forgiving yourself. You can open up the door to your soul by exploring the fullness of self-forgiveness. Learn from your mistakes, but don't spend your time unnecessarily punishing yourself for them. Accept the frailty of your own humanity, but let that acceptance make you more merciful to others and tolerant of their humanity. **Judge not, so that you are not judged.** You can embrace your own limitations without compromising your self-esteem in any way. The Lord, your Shepherd, prepares a table for you in the presence of your enemies, and you can be sure that even though He knows all your secrets, He will never tell them to the people on the other side of the table. Your secrets are safe with Him, and you can forgive yourself because He has forgiven you.

10.
You Can Live Your Life in the Now

Whatever you do in your life, don't miss, overlook, or underestimate the awesome power of the present. **This is the day the Lord has made; We will rejoice and be glad in it.** You must realize that this moment is so very beautiful and important and significant. You have to make every effort to seize the day – *this* day – and all of its opportunities, because there is really no such thing as an ordinary day. Every day matters. Every moment has potential. Every second contains unlimited possibilities. The Lord is your Shepherd, so you can live your life in the eternal "now." **NOW faith is.** The Shepherd reveals Himself to you as the *I AM*, not the "I Was" or the "I Will Be." **They that come to God must believe that HE IS.** Never, *ever,* allow your regret over the past, or your anxiety about the future, to rob you of the majesty of this moment. This moment is completely unique. This moment is yours.

Be thankful for what you have, but never let anything *have* you. You can own things without ever letting those things own you. Living in the now means that your identity is in who you are, not in the things that you have acquired. Living in the now means that you go with the flow of the seasons of your life: **To everything there is a season.** And when you come to the end of a good season, don't cry that it's over but, rather, smile because it happened. Living in the now means completely enjoying your moment in the sun and embracing the reality of when that moment has passed with true grace. Living in the now means you always know that you still have time left because your concept of the now triumphs over the limitations of time. The Lord is your Shepherd, so you can do something right now, with an optimistic attitude and with great vision. Hold on to your dream . . . God is in the now!

TWENTY-THREE

Part Seven Notes / A Time of Vindication

PART EIGHT: A Time of Prosperity

You Anoint My Head with Oil; My Cup Runs Over

The Lord shepherds me; I shall never be in need.

He gives me renewed life. He guides me along a virtuous course in accordance with His nature.

Your strength and support
are indeed my comfort.

You anoint my head with oil;
my fortunes prosper greatly.

Goodness and love alone will accompany me
through life, and I shall live in the house
of the Lord all my days.

Psalm 23 – The Psalms for Today:
A New Translation from the Hebrew
into Current English (R. K. Harrison)

TWENTY-THREE

1.
You Have an Anointing

You have an anointing from the Holy One, and you know all things. The Lord, your Shepherd, has, Himself, anointed your head with the oil of the Holy Spirit and supernaturally set you apart for a certain calling and a particular purpose. His anointing in and on your life empowers you by giving you a peculiar bent that can potentially be of great service to the Kingdom of God and to humanity in general. ***God anointed Jesus of Nazareth with the Holy Spirit and with power, who went about doing good.*** The talents, skills and abilities that He has invested within you, together with the desires that He has personally placed in your heart to do something meaningful with your life, are all a part of the equipping with which He has qualified you and the way in which He has enabled you to be effective in the earth. ***The Spirit of the Lord is upon me, because the Lord has anointed me.***

The Lord, your Shepherd, anoints your head with oil so that you will be able to walk through the valley of the shadow of death with absolutely no fear of evil. Fear can only prevent you from validating your anointing if you choose to allow it to do so. He anoints you at the table that He prepares for you in the presence of your enemies, so they will know that you are His and that they cannot remove the oil from your head, because they saw Him apply it to you there. He anoints your head with oil so that you will have all you need mentally, emotionally, spiritually and in every other way to live your best life. It's the anointing that makes the difference. ***The anointing which you have received from Him abides in you, and you do not need that anyone teach you; but as the anointing teaches you concerning all things, and is true, and is not a lie, and just as it has taught you, you will abide in Him.*** Selah!

2.
You Have Help

You are not alone. You are not helpless and you have not been abandoned. The Lord, your Shepherd, has not left you vulnerable or without resources, because He, Himself, has anointed your head with oil – the oil of gladness, the oil of favor, the oil of the anointing that produces real results. God is for you. **What shall we say then to these things? If God is for us, who can be against us?** Jesus ever lives to make intercession for you and the Helper, the Holy Spirit, has been sent into your life to stand by you in every minute of every day, to provide aid, assistance and comfort to you. **You shall receive power after that the Holy Spirit has come upon you.** You have partnership, whether in a spouse or a close friend. **Two are better than one . . . for if they fall, one will lift up his companion.** One can put a thousand enemies to flight, but two can do the very same to ten thousand enemies.

You have a community – a family, a local manifestation of the Body of Christ – where you have access to the help of apostles, prophets, evangelists, pastors and teachers. And if you invest in the relationships available to you in a local church body, you have the power to make a withdrawal from those same relationships. When you walk in covenant with others, you will find that people are more than willing to help out if they know the need. **Now are you the body of Christ, and members individually.** Open your eyes and realize that you have a support system and that you can make a demand on it when you need help. You have agreement, assistance and affirmation, and the relationships in your personal world cause your cup of life to run over. They enable you to tap into the Helper, Himself. The Lord is your Shepherd, you do not lack help and you are not out there on your own. You are connected. You are loved.

3.
You Have Abundant Life

Rejoice! You are alive! You have lived to see another beautiful day! You have breath in your lungs and blood pumping through your veins. You have awareness and identity and the joy of knowing that you have struggled to survive and you are still here. **His divine power has given us all things that pertain to life and godliness.** Your head is anointed with oil because it contains a living mind, and your cup of life runs over because the Shepherd gives to the sheep that faithfully follow Him the ability to thrive and prosper. The resurrected Lord is the originator and sustainer of all living things through His Spirit, and He who is the firstborn from the dead has eradicated the sting of death and has removed the victory of the grave. **If the Spirit of Him who raised Jesus from the dead dwells in you, He who raised Christ from the dead will also give life to your mortal bodies through His Spirit who dwells in you.**

The Lord, your Shepherd, reveals Himself to you through many covenant personalities, identified by many different covenant names that display the unlimited facets of His nature. One of those names in the Hebrew language is *El Shaddai: the God Who is More Than Enough.* In His incarnation as Jesus, the Christ, He said, **"I have come that they might have life, and that they might have it more abundantly."** You have the promise of a potentially beautiful existence, with unlimited freedom to explore every possibility available to you, through the life-giving power of the God who is *more than enough.* He has introduced a new law into the universe: the law of life. **The law of the Spirit of life in Christ Jesus has made me free from the law of sin and death.** God is real, God is alive and, through the power of His eternal Spirit, He has made you fully, eternally alive, as well.

4.
You Are Blessed

The Lord is your Shepherd and He has blessed you so that you can be a blessing. **All these blessings shall come upon you and overtake you, because you obey the voice of the Lord your God.** Your cup runs over because His blessings are overtaking you . . . coming upon you suddenly, even when you least expect it. **Blessed shall you be in the city, and blessed shall you be in the country.** Wherever the Shepherd leads you, you will be blessed on your journey. **Blessed shall be the fruit of your body, the produce of your ground.** Whatever you create will be blessed and whatever seeds you plant will grow and flourish. **Blessed shall you be when you come in, and blessed shall you be when you go out.** He anoints your head with oil so that you will be blessed when you enter a situation and blessed when you exit that same situation. You will be fortunate and highly favored in every circumstance.

Because the Shepherd prepares a table before you in the presence of your enemies, they will possibly think that you are just lucky because you lead a seemingly charmed life. They will most likely resent your blessed existence and be envious of the special light that shines on you. But you will know that your prosperous and auspicious lifestyle, with all of its promise and advantage, is the direct result of following the Shepherd into evergreen pastures. **The Lord will cause your enemies who rise against you to be defeated before your face; they shall come out against you one way and flee before you seven ways.** Because you are blessed, you can make it through the worst storms imaginable without hurt or damage. **The Lord will make you the head and not the tail; you shall be above only, and not be beneath.** He anoints your head with oil every day; your cup runs over all the days of your life.

5.
You Will Increase

The Lord, your Shepherd, anoints your head with oil. He anoints you for increase so that your cup of blessing and productivity is filled to overflowing. **May the Lord give you increase more and more, you and your children. May you be blessed by the Lord Who made heaven and earth.** The law of increase is built into you. You are hardwired to flourish and grow so that you can take dominion in the earth, be fruitful, and multiply. **God blessed them, and God said to them, "Be fruitful and multiply; fill the earth and subdue it; have dominion."** It is an aberration for you to diminish or regress, because all living things were meant to grow; all living things have the law of Genesis working in them. As you follow the Shepherd, you will naturally be enlarged and stretched and extended. He leads you to the pastures beyond your familiar comfort zones so that you can have more.

Expand your vision. Increase your capacity for faith as you fight the good fight against the limitations of human reasoning day by day. **Enlarge the place of your tent, and let them stretch out the curtains of your dwellings; Do not spare; Lengthen your cords, and strengthen your stakes.** Prepare for more in your life by visualizing and vocalizing your great expectations, charging the atmosphere around you with possibilities by the words of your mouth. To create an atmosphere of expectancy is to prepare yourself to experience the miraculous. **You shall expand to the right and to the left, and your descendants will inherit the nations, and make the desolate cities inhabited.** All things are possible with God, but you must reach the level where you can walk in the reality of that little by little, one step at a time. You may increase incrementally, but you will definitely increase. Get ready . . . *the future is now!*

6.
You Can Be in the Flow

The Lord is your Shepherd; your cup of prosperity runs over. One word that is often associated with prosperity is the word *affluent,* and the word *affluent* comes from the same root as the word *flow.* It means the flow of wealth, the flow of increase, the flow of blessing, the flow that is available to you as the Shepherd leads you beside the still waters. The oil with which the Shepherd anoints your head is growing into a mighty river of anointing – the river of God merging with the river of your life. **He shall be like a tree planted by the rivers of water, that brings forth its fruit in its season, whose leaf shall not wither; And whatsoever he does shall prosper.** A flow of finances and provision is yours – a flow of favor and potential success where every vision is realized and manifested, every wish is granted, every prayer is answered in the affirmative, and every dream comes true.

The wind blows where it wishes, and you hear the sound of it, but cannot tell where it comes from and where it goes. So is everyone who is born of the Spirit. Being in the flow means freeing yourself to walk in the Spirit, without permitting the rigidity of religious bias or prejudice to box you in or cause you to fear transition or resist change. It means being willing to think in a new way and allowing the Shepherd to supernaturally guide you with and by an inward witness. It means following the path of peace to a place where you make good decisions that will bring you satisfaction and a sense of accomplishment. Being in the flow means being sensitive to be led to the right place at the right time to meet the right people for the right reasons so that you can do the right thing. **The steps of a good man are ordered by the Lord, and He delights in His way.** You are affluent. You are in the flow.

7.
You Are Going to Prosper

Jesus Christ . . . though He was rich, yet for your sakes He became poor, that you through His poverty might become rich. The Lord is your Shepherd, and He fills your cup to overflowing, causing you to prosper in a healthy, life-affirming way. *The blessing of the Lord makes rich, and He adds no sorrow with it.* You are anointed to be a blessing to humanity . . . to use your prosperity to make a positive difference in your community. You are anointed to acquire wealth so that you may be able to improve your environment, ultimately making the world in which you live a better place. You are anointed to succeed in all the affairs of life so that you can be an asset to the Kingdom of God and help to establish His covenant in the earth. *You shall remember the Lord your God, for it is He who gives you the power to get wealth, that He may establish His covenant which He swore to your fathers.*

The Shepherd anoints your *head* – the source of your thinking and intelligence – with His oil, because prosperity has to do with the way you think, with your mental perception of things. *Beloved, I pray that you may prosper in all things and be in health, just as your soul prospers.* The prosperity of the soul is the prosperity of the mind and prosperity, just like poverty, is an attitude – an *internal* paradigm that eventually manifests itself in your life *externally*. Being broke or without funds is a temporary condition that has no connection to poverty. If your cup is running over, you cannot be poor. The Lord, your Shepherd, knows where the greenest pastures are, and the table that He prepares for you holds a banquet fit for kings. *Let them shout for joy and be glad, who favor my righteous cause; And let them say continually, "Let the Lord be magnified, who has pleasure in the prosperity of His servant."*

8.
You Are Going to Succeed

This book of the law shall not depart from your mouth, but you shall meditate in it day and night, that you may observe to do according to all that is written in it. For then you will make your way prosperous, and then you will have good success. The Lord, your Shepherd, will never lead you into failure. It is His will and intention that you have and continually experience success in everything that you set your mind to do . . . that you make good on everything you set your hand to . . . that you thrive and prosper through the good times and the bad. He has anointed your head with oil so that you can flourish, regardless of your circumstances or location, and so you may progress and continue to advance until you win. You must succeed so that you can be effective for the Kingdom and bear fruit in the material world. You are anointed to accomplish the thing for which you aim, and you may always expect a favorable outcome.

God has smiled on you, so good fortune is yours. He has commanded a blessing on all your achievements and He rejoices over your triumphs. You are anointed to be victorious. Your cup runs over in a way that is continually profitable for you, so you have the potential to be wealthy and to make yourself rich. It doesn't matter what has happened in the past; your past is no indicator of your future. And regardless of how things currently look, you must make the decision to rejoice and to remain positive, and continue to praise the Lord. ***Though the fig tree may not blossom, nor fruit be on the vines; Though the labor of the olive may fail, and the fields yield no food; Though the flock be cut off from the stalls - Yet I will rejoice in the God of my salvation. The Lord God is my strength; He will make my feet like deer's feet, and He will make me walk on my high hills.*** Success is possible; go for it!

9.
You're Not Going to Lose Everything

Your cup runs over, so you don't have to feel fearful or paranoid about the possibility of losing what you potentially have to lose. The Lord, your Shepherd, provides full protection for you and all your possessions, and He is watching over you at all times to make sure your life is preserved. **I will rebuke the devourer for your sake, so that he will not destroy the fruit of your ground, nor shall the vine fail to bear fruit for you in the field.** Don't accept a negative report that tries to convince you that you are going to lose your prosperity, and don't believe everything you hear about hard times and bad things to come. **The threshing floors shall be full of wheat, and the vats shall overflow with new wine and oil. So I will restore to you the years that the swarming locust has eaten . . . you shall eat in plenty and be satisfied.** When you are actively following the Shepherd, you don't have time to hear bad news.

It all belongs to God anyway, and whatever you had within you that attracted prosperity or things to you in the first place is still within you. When you seek first the Kingdom of God and His righteousness, the things you need are added to you, and you may have those things without those things ever having you. You are not your possessions, so you must always keep them in perspective in regard to your identity. You are not what you *have;* you are who you *are*. **Therefore I say to you, do not worry about your life, what you will eat or what you will drink; not about your body, what you will put on. Is not life more than food and the body more than clothing?** The Shepherd leads you into green pastures where you can consider the lilies of the field and appreciate the fact that they do not toil or spin. Don't worry about anything. The same God who gives all good gifts has given you a spirit of love and of power and of a sound mind.

10.
You Will Have More Than Enough

The Lord, your Shepherd, anoints your head with oil so that you will always have more than enough. You literally are *anointed for prosperity.* **Oh, fear the Lord, you His saints! There is no want or lack to those who fear Him.** Following the Shepherd always leads you to fertile, green pastures where you may eat until you are full. **The young lions lack and suffer hunger; But those who seek the Lord shall not lack any good thing.** There is no lack in the universe, there is only a problem with distribution and that problem is solved for you when you learn how to perceive things correctly. **What man is there among you who, if his son asks for bread, will give him a stone? Or if he asks for a fish, will he give him a serpent? If you then, being evil, know how to give good gifts to your children, how much more will your Father who is in heaven give good things to those who ask Him!**

The Lord, your Shepherd, knows what you need even before you ask, and He is very committed to your total and complete provision. He doesn't just fill your cup – He causes your cup to run over! He doesn't just give you good measure – He gives to you good measure, pressed down, shaken together and running over! He doesn't just do what you think He will do – He does exceedingly abundantly above all that you can ask or think! **The Lord God is a sun and shield; The Lord will give grace and glory; No good thing will He withhold from those who walk uprightly.** The Lord is your Shepherd, you shall not want . . . you shall not lack . . . you shall not go without . . . you shall not have less than . . . you shall not lose out . . . you shall not be deficient . . . you shall not be destitute . . . you shall not fall short . . . you shall not experience scarcity . . . you shall not go hungry. El Shaddai knows where you are and what you need.

TWENTY-THREE

Part Eight Notes / A Time of Prosperity

PART NINE: A Time of Progress

Surely Goodness and Mercy Shall Follow Me All the Days of My Life

The Lord is my Shepherd; I shall want nothing.

He makes me lie down in green pastures,
and leads me beside the waters of peace;
He renews life within me, and for his name's sake
guides me in the right path.

Even though I walk through a valley dark as death,
I fear no evil, for thou art with me,
thy staff and thy crook are my comfort.

Thou spreadest a table for me in the sight of my
enemies; Thou has richly bathed my head
with oil, and my cup runs over.

Goodness and love unfailing,
these will follow me all the days of my life,
and I shall dwell in the house of the Lord
my whole life long.

Psalm 23 – The New English Bible

1.
Your Life Has a Purpose

Your life has a purpose – a unique and valuable purpose that is unfolding and coming into better focus every day of your life as you become more and more comfortable in your own skin by submitting to His uniquely perfect will for your personal life. **Whom He foreknew, He also predestined to be conformed to the image of His Son, that He might be the firstborn among many brethren.** You are not aimlessly floating through life as the product of random biology. You are not here by accident. There is something for you to do that *only* you can do. You must live your own life, not the life that someone else thinks you should live. You must fulfill the will of God for you, not the will of someone else who wants to impose his or her agenda on you. When you believe in your purpose, you empower yourself to continually seek higher ground and to attain your goals, level by level. Your purpose helps you to develop a plan.

The Lord, your Shepherd, has carefully designed your personal path where goodness and mercy may follow you all the days of your life to help bring you into your destiny. And the fact that goodness and mercy are *following* you is an indication that you are moving. **In Him we live, and move, and have our being.** The fact that you are *moving* is an indication that you are going somewhere. And if you are going somewhere, you are making progress – you are progressing in your thinking, in your self-perception, and in your lifestyle. Make every day count, because nothing you do for the Kingdom of God or for the betterment of the world around you is wasted. It all counts for something . . . it all means something . . . it all matters. **My beloved brethren, be steadfast, immovable, always abounding in the work of the Lord, knowing that your labor is not in vain in the Lord.**

2.
You Have the Grace of God

The grace of God is on your life. It always has been, which is why all things have worked together for your good. God has graced you to be who you are so that you can do what you do. **But by the grace of God I am what I am, and His grace toward me was not in vain; but I labored more abundantly than they all, yet not I, but the grace of God which was with me.** The grace of God has always been there for you, equipping you to do things that you thought you could never do (yet you did them), and that abundant grace is still available to you to empower you to accomplish the tasks ahead of you that seem impossible today. Grace is a gift, and goodness and mercy follow you every day of your life because they are activated by that grace, that unmerited favor of God. The Lord, your Shepherd, has chosen a path of grace on which to lead you. His grace has brought you safely this far and His grace will lead you home.

You were saved by the grace of God, and your salvation is ongoing and perpetual; you are literally *being* saved every day of your life. **By grace you have been saved through faith, and that not of yourselves; it is the gift of God, not of works, lest anyone should boast.** God's grace has been granted to you for a specific purpose, and that purpose defines you as His workmanship, His personal masterpiece. **We are His workmanship, created in Christ Jesus for good works, which God prepared beforehand that we should walk in them.** Don't dread the future. The grace of God that has brought you through, time and time again, will be there for you tomorrow. Cross each bridge when you get to it, knowing that there is a gift of grace there that will get you from one side to the other. You are gifted. You are equipped. You are able. You are anointed. You are empowered. You are graced.

3.
You Have the Mercy of God

God's mercy endures forever, and it's a powerful force that keeps your right standing with God intact, regardless of your shortcomings and weaknesses. **Through the Lord's mercies we are not consumed, because His compassions fail not. They are new every morning; Great is your faithfulness.** Every morning when you wake up, there is a fresh supply of mercy available to you to get you through that day. His mercy, along with His undeniable goodness, follows you . . . every day . . . all the days of your life. You didn't do anything to deserve His great mercy and you can't do anything to lose it or to make it go away. It is even on your children's children, working on behalf of generations yet to be born. **The mercy of the Lord is from everlasting to everlasting on those who fear him, and His righteousness to children's children.** The mercy of God is much bigger and broader than the scope of your life.

The Lord is merciful and gracious, slow to anger, and abounding in mercy. He will not always strive with us, nor will He keep His anger forever. The Lord, your Shepherd, leads you in paths of righteousness, which are paths of His mercy, not for the preservation of your reputation, but for *His* name's sake. **I, even I, am he who blots out your transgressions for my own sake; and I will not remember your sins.** Surely . . . definitely . . . absolutely . . . without a doubt . . . goodness and mercy shall follow you all the days of your life. God is good and God is merciful, even to a thousand generations. If His mercy endures forever, then you can be assured that there is enough of it for you today to get you through. **He has not dealt with us according to our sins, nor punished us according to our iniquities. For as the heavens are high above the earth, so great is His mercy toward those who fear Him.**

4.
You Have the Favor of God

Let not mercy and truth forsake you; Bind them around your neck, write them on the tablet of your heart, and so find favor and high esteem in the sight of God and man. The Lord is your Shepherd; you have an edge – a supernatural advantage – called *favor* that transcends human personal relationships and causes people to help you rise to the top, even if they don't want to or even realize that they are doing so. Favor with God is a given because He loves you unconditionally. But favor with people is something that is beyond reason, because God will cause people to give you favor who don't necessarily even like you all that much. Favor will cause your enemies to reward and promote you, even to celebrate you! ***When a man's ways please the Lord, he makes even his enemies to be at peace with him.*** Favor sets you in a large place and causes you to lead a charmed life. Favor is power.

For you, O lord, will bless the righteous; With favor You will surround him as with a shield. Favor – the touch of blessing from heaven – protects you from harm and guarantees that ***no weapon formed against you will prosper*** and that ***every tongue that rises against you in judgment shall be shown to be in the wrong.*** Favor: it's all over you and around you, giving you an advantage in relationships, in business, and in all the affairs of life. The favor of God enables you to enjoy your own prosperity and success and to see the fulfillment of your dreams. It allows you to derive real pleasure from the quality relationships in your life without becoming co-dependant on or with them. Favor makes it possible for you to overcome obstacles and do the impossible so that you are able to look at the life you have created through your faith and say, as God said in His review of His creation, "It is good!"

TWENTY-THREE

5.
You Have the Forgiveness of God

God is not mad at you. He reconciled you to Himself in the cross, so you don't need to exist under a cloud of imagined guilt or be alienated from Him in your mind. You have His unconditional love and acceptance because goodness and mercy follow you all the days of your life. **He was wounded for our transgressions, He was bruised for our iniquities; The chastisement of our peace was upon Him, and by His stripes we are healed.** God has forgiven you. God was in Christ reconciling the world to Himself, and you are a partaker of that miraculous act. **All we like sheep have gone astray; We have turned, every one, to his own way; And the Lord has laid on Him the iniquity of us all.** God is good and His mercy endures forever. Every day of your life, as you follow the Lord, your Shepherd, you must also see Him as the Lamb of God who takes away the sin of the world.

Because Jesus was crucified from the world's foundation, and because you were chosen in Him to be holy and without blame at that time, you were forgiven before you got here, long before you ever did anything that needed forgiveness. But, so that you may take responsibility for your own life and actions and so that your heart does not condemn you before Him and you lose your confidence, you have this promise on which to stand: **If we confess our sins, He is faithful and just to forgive us our sins and to cleanse us from all unrighteousness.** But this promise must be kept in context, in proportion to the larger picture of God's mercy to all: **These things I write to you, so that you may not sin. And if anyone sins, we have an Advocate with the Father, Jesus Christ . . . He Himself is the propitiation for our sins, and not for ours only but also FOR THE WHOLE WORLD.** The Lord is your Shepherd; you are forgiven.

6.
You Can Be Happy

It's OK to be happy. **The joy of the Lord is your strength.** Happiness is not joy, but happiness is important and it is attainable and can definitely be maintained. Because it is an attitude – a state of mind and a daily decision – happiness can be developed into a Kingdom lifestyle. **These things I have spoken to you, that in Me you may have peace; In the world you will have tribulation; but be of good cheer, I have overcome the world.** Happiness is available and reachable regardless of how much unhappiness you have experienced in the past. **When the Lord brought back the captivity of Zion, we were like those who dream. Then our mouth was filled with laughter and our tongue with singing.** All things are possible. You can have a happy life, because goodness and mercy follow you all the days of your life, even in a world that seems to be filled with pain and sorrow.

A merry heart does good, like medicine, but a broken spirit dries the bones. Happiness creates health and prolongs life. *A merry heart makes a cheerful countenance, but by sorrow of heart the spirit is broken.* When you are internally happy, you cause the negative circumstances in your life to turn around, forcing them to yield to the power of your merry heart. *All the days of the afflicted are evil, but he who is of a merry heart has a continual feast.* That "continual feast" is the table which the Lord prepares for you in the presence of your enemies, even the enemies of your own negative thoughts and emotions. Because the Lord is your Shepherd, you can stop being your own worst enemy and put an end to your tendency to work against yourself. Godly happiness brings your internal world into harmony and order so that you can be a friend to yourself. God is good. Be happy!

TWENTY-THREE

7.
You Can Enjoy Your Life

There is beauty and grace in every single minute of every single day if you learn how to look for it and recognize it when you see it. There is always something to be happy about, even in the midst of the worst and most trying times of your life. There really is a silver lining to every dark cloud and a happy ending to every chapter of the book of your life. ***I know that nothing is better for them than to rejoice and to do good in their lives, and also that every man should eat and drink and enjoy the good of all his labor - it is the gift of God.*** There's still so much to look forward to, so much good left to be done in your life. Goodness and mercy have been following you all the days of your life, so there is no experience that is wasted, no bitter memory that can't be turned into an overcoming testimony. You have learned lessons from your mistakes and now you can enjoy the wisdom that you have acquired.

Weeping may endure for the night, but joy comes in the morning. No matter how much pain and heartache you have experienced in your lifetime, you can put it all in perspective and put it behind you. That was then, this is now. Choose to be happy. It is God's will that you learn to enjoy your life, your ministry, and your relationships. You can begin a new chapter where you appreciate nature – the beauty of God's creation – and learn to enjoy your own company enough that you can spend time alone with yourself and be content somewhere in that creation. You don't have to be perfect to be happy, and the circumstances of your life don't have to be perfect for you to enjoy them. Be thankful and optimistic. Develop a vision for happiness and hold on to it, always remembering that you must enjoy things inwardly before you can enjoy them in the material world. Most of all, enjoy the presence of the Lord, your Shepherd.

8.
You Are Making Progress

You're doing better than you think you are. Step by step you are moving toward your goal, climbing a little higher each day as you make peace with your life and put away the childish things that impede your progress. **Being confident of this very thing, that He who has begun a good work in you will complete it until the day of Jesus Christ.** One thing is for sure, you've come too far to give up now! Don't underestimate the progress that you have made and don't ever think about quitting. Don't give up on yourself. Determine to keep moving forward, regardless of discouragement or any feelings of being overwhelmed with your responsibilities. Goodness and mercy are following you all the days of your life, so you must continue to face forward. Never look back; these are the good days and you have everything to look forward to. Give God the glory for your progress and reward yourself for *your* efforts, as well.

Maintain a positive attitude about your own progress, even when you encounter what seems to be a setback in your life. You must maintain a genuine confidence and good feeling about the direction that your life is taking. **Do not cast away your confidence, which has great reward. For you have need of endurance, so that after you have done the will of God, you may receive the promise.** Determine to always see your glass as being half-full, rather than half-empty. Don't waste your time complaining or worrying. Both things are counterproductive time-wasters. **The just shall live by faith; But if anyone draws back, My soul has no pleasure in him.** The Lord, your Shepherd, is leading you to higher ground, greener pastures, and to a greater understanding that you are exactly where you need to be on your path right now. You're doing fine. Keep up the good work!

9.
Your Path Is Growing Brighter

You are on a journey – an ongoing adventure in God – where every day gets a little better as your path grows a little brighter, leading you through one open door after another. ***The path of the just is like the shining sun, that shines ever brighter unto the perfect day.*** The Shepherd is leading you on a path that requires you to be uncompromisingly just, because His righteousness in you is like the light of dawn – it shines more and more and becomes brighter and clearer until it reaches its full strength and glory. Don't waste your time on regrets or in wondering what might have been, what could have been, or what should have been. Don't second-guess anything that has happened. Embrace your whole path, with all of its ups and downs, hills and valleys, and determine not to wish that you could change anything about it. Look back over the path you have traveled and say, "It is what it is, and it's all good!"

He shall be like the light of the morning when the sun rises, a morning without clouds, like the tender grass springing out of the earth, by clear shining after the rain. Goodness and mercy follow you all the days of your life, and they are always there behind you doing clean up on the messes you have made and damage control for the fallout from your less-than-perfect decisions. It doesn't matter that you have fallen short: ***A righteous man may fall seven times and rise again.*** You can get back up again when you fall. You can get right back on that path that was growing brighter before you got off of it and find that the light of God is still shining on it. Your mistake was not the end of the world. Get it in perspective. Stop dwelling on it. Move on. Today is a new day and there is a wonderful path waiting for you. The Lord, your Shepherd, is on that path ahead of you and all He asks is that you follow Him.

10.
You Can Fulfill Your Destiny

You can and should be proud of your life, no matter what has happened in your past and regardless of your present circumstances. You can live a progressive existence and leave a great legacy behind you by fulfilling your own unique destiny. **For whom He foreknew, He also predestined to be conformed to the image of His Son, that He might be the firstborn among many brethren.** God has a wonderful plan for your life that is ultimately for the sole purpose of leading you to being conformed to the image of Christ. The Shepherd does not lead you just for the sake of leading. He is actually taking you somewhere, and goodness and mercy are following you all the days of your life to make sure that you get there. **I press on, that I may lay hold of that for which Christ Jesus has also laid hold of me . . . I press toward the goal for the prize of the upward call of God in Christ Jesus.**

God knew you *before* you got here, before you were born. You existed before you experienced earthly existence and your destiny was already in place: **Before I formed you in the womb I knew you; Before you were born I sanctified you.** You are an eternal being; your destiny is important and is a part of the grand scheme of things. Fulfilling that destiny brings inner peace and joy unspeakable, full of glory. You were born to be His dwelling place, destined to bring pleasure to God. **You are worthy, O Lord . . . For you created all things, and by your will they exist and were created.** You have a destiny to fulfill that is yours alone. You can't do it by yourself – you will need the help of others. But at the end of the day, you are accountable for your own life and for how you tried to make it everything that it could be. You are responsible to maximize your potential – without excuses and without comparisons to others.

TWENTY-THREE

Part Nine Notes / A Time of Progress

PART TEN: A Time of Fulfillment

I Will Dwell in the House of the Lord Forever

> Because the Lord is my Shepherd,
> I have everything I need!
>
> He lets me rest in the meadow grass and leads me
> beside the quiet streams.
> He restores my failing health.
> He helps me do what honors him the most.
>
> Even when walking through the dark valley of death
> I will not be afraid, for you are close beside me,
> guarding, guiding all the way.
>
> You provide delicious food for me in the presence of
> my enemies. You have welcomed me as your guest;
> blessings overflow!
>
> Your goodness and unfailing kindness shall be with
> me all of my life, and afterwards
> I will live with you forever in your home.
>
> Psalm 23 – Living Bible

TWENTY-THREE

1.
You Are in the Family of God

The Lord is your Shepherd and you will dwell in His house forever. He leads you in the paths of righteousness because you are called to bridge the perceived gap between the family of man and the family of God, being a proactive resident of both the city of man and the city of God. **For this reason I bow my knees to the Father of our Lord Jesus Christ, from whom the whole family in heaven and earth is named.** Your Father is a doting parent who has surrounded you with love and has lavished upon you all the personal attention that you need, all the while embracing the families and peoples of the whole earth. The God who rules the nations has also secured your life with full proof that you are loved, appreciated and cared for. You are not alone; you are family. **You did not receive the spirit of bondage again to fear, but you received the Spirit of adoption, by whom we cry out "Abba, Father!"**

No one goes hungry in the house of God – **My God shall supply all your need according to His riches in glory by Christ Jesus** – and no one is without shelter, warmth, or companionship. The Father provides for His family. And even though, as the Shepherd, He disciplines and even chastens you when necessary, He also pampers and spoils you whenever possible. **I am the good shepherd. The good shepherd gives His life for the sheep.** The Shepherd will be good and faithful to you all the days of your life. **He will feed His flock like a shepherd; He will gather the lambs with His arm, and carry them in His bosom, and gently lead those who are with young.** The Lord is your Shepherd and you will dwell in His house forever. You will know Him intimately because He is also your closest kin. **I am the good shepherd; and I know My sheep, and am known by My own.**

2.
You Are Welcome in the House of God

One thing have I desired of the Lord, that will I seek: That I may dwell in the house of the Lord all the days of my life, to behold the beauty of the Lord and to inquire in His temple. For in the time of trouble He shall hide me in His pavilion; In the secret place of His tabernacle He shall hide me; He shall set me high upon a rock. You have the promise of total fulfillment – the kind of fulfillment that only comes from having a sense of place, a sense of belonging. Goodness and mercy follow you all the days of your life to remind you that you have a place in God. You belong. In God, you are home. In your understanding of His loving nature and personal relationship to you, you have a permanent welcome, an eternal open-door policy. His arms are open to you at all times. His ears are attentive to your every call. In His presence you will find rest for your weary soul. There is peace in the warmth of His house.

You have been welcomed into a great big house where every child of God is cared for and celebrated. **Do not fear, little flock, for it is your Father's good pleasure to give you the Kingdom.** There will always be a room for you in the Father's house, because Jesus Himself prepared one just for you. You are an integral part of His household of faith: **As we have opportunity, let us do good to all, especially to those who are of the household of faith.** He has welcomed you into His eternal presence by offering you an unbreakable covenant, and His righteousness is now your residence, as your heart is His home. You are in Him and He is in you. You live in Him as He lives in you. You're not just a guest or tenant – you are absolutely in the very bloodline and royal lineage of the Creator Himself! You bear the family name. You are a part of the divine dynasty – the dynasty of God!

TWENTY-THREE

3.
You Can Be at Peace Anywhere

The peace that passes understanding – the peace that supersedes all intellect or logic – is an internal phenomenon that is a gift from the Lord, your Shepherd, Himself. **Peace I leave with you.** It originates in the secret place of the Most High and it flows from your heart, through your mind and emotions, until it permeates your very existence, making you righteousness-conscious and comfortable in your own skin. **My peace I give to you; not as the world gives do I give you. Let not your heart be troubled, neither let it be afraid.** The green pastures and still waters spoken of by the Psalmist are in your mind, in your thoughts, in your internal world, and you have the authority to refuse to let your heart be afraid, nervous, anxious or agitated. **You will keep him in perfect peace whose mind is stayed on you.** Because you know that you will dwell in the house of the Lord forever, you can be at peace anywhere.

The Kingdom of God is not meat and drink. The Kingdom of God is not rules and regulations about eating and drinking or anything else that is external or religious. God's Kingdom is comprised of **righteousness, PEACE, and joy in the Holy Spirit.** The peaceful Kingdom of God is internal. **The Kingdom of God does not come by observation,** and that peace is only manifested in the material world as the Word becomes flesh in every individual life. The Lord is your Shepherd, so you can be comfortable wherever you are and can find contentment in whatever state you find yourself. You never have to feel disoriented or homesick, because you're not limited to natural geography or finite definitions of location. God is everywhere and you are in Him, so you can be happy and relaxed and serene anywhere and everywhere that you go as you follow the leading of the Good Shepherd.

4.
You Can Love Yourself

The two great commandments that Jesus said made the law of the Old Covenant obsolete are really three commandments: **Jesus said to him, "You shall love the Lord your God with all your heart, with all your soul, and with all your mind." This is the first and great commandment. And the second is like it: "You shall love your neighbor AS YOU LOVE YOURSELF."** The third commandment – the commandment to *love yourself* – is implied here. It is taken for granted in Jesus' revolutionary words concerning the operation of His new world order that self-love is the standard by which love for others is measured. The love for a "neighbor" (which is practically given equal importance to the love for God), is to be in direct proportion to the love for self. The Lord is your Shepherd, so you can be free to love yourself without reservation and enjoy dwelling in His house – the house that love built – forever.

Love in the Christ-Kingdom is the ultimate revelation. **Beloved, let us love one another, for love is of God, and EVERYONE WHO LOVES is born of God, and knows God. He who does not love does not know God, for God is love.** According to the Apostle's amazing words, the manifestation of love is the evidence of God-birth, and the only way to know God is through the revelation of love. Unconditional love for Kingdom neighbors begins with unconditional love and acceptance of self. You cannot follow the Shepherd and dwell in His house forever without loving others, and you must love them *as you love yourself*. God's love is the origin of all things: **we love Him because He first loved us.** He makes you lie down in green pastures because He loves you. He leads you beside the still waters because He loves you. He anoints your head with oil because He loves you. God is love.

5.
You Have the Nature of God

It's all in you – the very nature of God Himself. You are His creation . . . His child . . . the offspring of the Divine Majesty. **As His divine power has given unto us all things that pertain to life and godliness . . . by which have been given to us exceedingly great and precious promises, that through these you may be partakers of the divine nature.** The children of God who know who they are and remember where they came from, are designed to live in this world at a higher altitude, existing in a more dynamic dimension. **That which is born of flesh is flesh, and that which is born of Spirit is spirit.** The ongoing experience of being born again enables the child of God to perceive the Kingdom, empowering him or her to walk in the Spirit where all things are possible. As you follow the Lord, your Shepherd, day by day, you too will clarify your spiritual identity and tap into your eternal root system and ancestry.

More importantly, those who know *why they are here* live in the ultimate consciousness and confidence. Specifically, you are born of God – **to as many as received Him, to them He gave the authority to become the sons of God** – and, as such, you are an exile from your true birthplace, an emissary from heaven sent to this planet to colonize it and claim it for the Homeland. Your understanding of the nature of God within you enables you to actively participate in helping to turn this current earth into a replica of heaven. It is why your garden-grandparents were put here in the first place: **Let us make man in our image, and let them have dominion.** The foundation of godly confidence is Spirit-revealed, righteousness-consciousness. Righteousness – right-standing with God – is ground zero for everything that you think and do, and the awareness of it comes from your belief that you will dwell in the house of the Lord forever.

6.
You Can Know the Will of God

Your mind and heart can be anchored in the absolute, bedrock confidence that you are moving in the right direction with your life because the Lord, your Shepherd, wants you to know His will more than *you* want to know it. **Your Kingdom come; Your will be done on earth as it is in heaven.** Little by little, the big plan – *the master plan* – is being revealed and distilled into your consciousness through regular acts of obedience that sometimes seem insignificant and unimportant. **Obedience is better than sacrifice.** As you develop the spiritual perception to walk out your destiny by faith – literally going "from faith to faith" – you will strengthen the capacity of your understanding heart or, better said, you will begin to manifest the Mind of Christ. God is speaking **line upon line; precept upon precept,** because your natural mind cannot accommodate the vastness of His full plan for your life.

Listen carefully to the still, small voice that speaks from within your inner sanctuary **(My sheep know my voice)** and pay attention to confirmation and signposts on the road to success that come to you as a word in season established by the mouth of two or three witnesses. Meditate on the dreams that He has placed within you, those seeds of destiny that are the planting of the Lord. **Delight yourself, also, in the Lord, and He will give you the desires of your heart.** Those ever-present desires that keep you motivated are gifts from God – hints from heaven, previews of the big picture that's being painted. And even though they sometimes frustrate you and sometimes cause you bewilderment, the very fact that they don't go away means that they have roots in eternity. Don't give up on them. Don't give up on the plan. Don't resent waiting on the will of God, because His burden is easy and His yoke is light.

7.
You Don't Have to Envy Anyone

The Lord, your Shepherd, is a loving and vigilant Caretaker/Provider who has offered you, and continues to offer you, personal security and the assurance that there will always be enough to go around. There is enough for you. *He* is enough for you; in fact, He's *more* than enough! **He that spared not His own Son, but delivered Him up for us all, how shall He not, with Him, freely give us all things?** Because all of the promises of God are "yes" and "amen," you can successfully live your own life and be thankful for all that you have while maintaining that all-important attitude of gratitude. Because He has anointed your head with oil and made your cup to run over, you have the possibility and probability of realizing all of your potential. It's all inside you **(the Kingdom of God is within you)**, so allowing yourself to envy someone else is a complete waste of your costly time. *Jehovah Jireh* is your provider.

You don't even have to compare yourself to someone else, because you are completely and amazingly unique. Jealousy and envy, and the feelings of inferiority and inadequacy that they produce, are negative, destructive forces that can never, *ever,* be tolerated in your life under any circumstances. You are you, and you are good enough – no better than anyone else, but no less valuable or important, either. **For love is as strong as death, jealousy as cruel as the grave; Its flames are flames of fire, a most vehement flame.** Your contribution to the world is as positive and necessary as anyone else's. You will dwell in the house of the Lord forever with your own room, your own place of significance, that will never be lost or taken for granted by the Lord, your Shepherd. So, don't be afraid that He will overlook you and give someone else the attention that you need and deserve. **There is no fear in love, but perfect love casts out fear.**

8.
You Can Have a Fulfilling Life

Don't fear your old age. Don't waste any time regretting the past. Don't be overly upset if everyone doesn't like you or approve of you. Don't envy anyone else's life. Never, *ever*, take your life for granted or wish it were over. Never even *consider* doing yourself any harm. **Because he has set his love upon Me, therefore I will deliver Him; I will set him on high because he has known my name.** No matter what is happening right now, enjoy this day and appreciate it for what it is. Be content with what you have. Count your blessings. The Lord, your Shepherd, wants you to live in His house forever! What do you have to be depressed about? All the usual clichés – *"Take it one day at a time," "Stop and smell the roses," "Whatever doesn't break you will make you," "Today is the first day of the rest of your life"* – still have meaning, resonance and relevance, because they are true, *and they are true for you!*

You can absolutely have a wonderful, fulfilling life when you know how to correctly see everything around you and when you remember to keep your eyes on the Shepherd and on the path that He has set before you. You can be happy right where you are, right now, with what you have. The Lord is your Shepherd, you shall not want. Don't let the external circumstances or present troubles faze you in the least. **He shall call upon Me, and I will answer him; I will be with him in trouble; I will deliver him and honor him.** In spite of how you feel at this very minute, you are still promised a fulfilling life, because God is good. Regardless of your current age, there is still time left to accomplish great things. You still have a lot of living left to do. **With long life I will satisfy him, and show him my salvation.** You are going from glory to glory to live a life that matters, a life that counts for something. Be happy. Be fulfilled.

9.
You Are in the Presence of God

You will show me the path of life; In Your presence is fullness of joy; At your right hand are pleasures forevermore. In the eternal presence of the Lord, your Shepherd, there is not just the fullness of joy, but there is a fullness of everything good and perfect. Every good and perfect gift that comes down from the Father of Lights brings fullness and abundance and security and wellness and wholeness to you. You are surrounded by His love – His eternal, life-giving, life-affirming and unconditional love. He is everywhere in your life: past, present and future. **Where can I go from Your Spirit? Or where can I flee from Your presence?** You were in Him before He laid the foundations of the world, and you will be in Him always and forever. No one can pluck you out of His hand, and nothing can ever take you out of His heart. **Who shall separate us from the love of God?** God is with you. God is in you. God is for you.

You can never hide from His presence and, more importantly, you never have to. No matter who tells you that you are "naked," you never need to scramble through the garden, desperately searching for leaves to sew together to hide yourself from His eyes. **Neither is there any creature that is not manifest in His sight: but all things are naked and opened unto the eyes of Him with whom we have to do.** Do not be alienated from God in your mind any longer; He has seen it all and He still thinks that you, His workmanship, are completely beautiful. **"Can anyone hide himself in secret places, So I shall not see him?" says the Lord; "Do I not fill heaven and earth?" says the Lord.** You are in the presence of Almighty God. **God is a Spirit, and they that worship Him must worship Him in spirit and in truth.** Worship Him in the Spirit; worship Him in your whole, uncensored truth.

10.
You Are Home

Please feel free to make yourself at home in the house of the Lord forever. ***In My Father's house are many rooms; if it were not so, I would have told you. I go to prepare a place for you.*** There is a place for you in God and that place transcends space and time. Your place is secure. You are significant to God. He wants you in His house, partaking of His economy and of the commonwealth of His family, His holy nation. ***He who dwells in the secret place of the Most High shall abide under the shadow of the Almighty.*** When you realize that you are home, you will experience the eternal goodness of God and you will never, *ever*, be alone. ***Behold, I stand at the door and knock. If anyone hears My voice and opens the door, I will come in to him and dine with him, and he with Me.*** You never have to fear the future or be uncertain about where you are going, because you will dwell in the house of the Lord forever.

The Lord is your Shepherd; you shall not lack a dwelling-place, ever. You are not homeless. You are not an orphan. You are not a stranger in a strange land. You are not a foreigner. You may follow the Shepherd as a pilgrim, but never as a rambler. When He makes you lie down in green pastures, He lies down with you, holding you securely in His warm embrace throughout the coldness of the night. When He leads you beside still waters, He watches over you to make sure that no predator hiding in the tall grass along the shoreline can get to you. When He restores your soul, He indelibly stamps on your mind a map of the road that leads home so that you can never get lost. The paths of righteousness in which He leads you always bring you full circle, back to your place of origin. ***If anyone loves Me, he will keep My word; and My Father will love him, and We will come to him and make Our home with him.*** There's no place like home.

TWENTY-THREE

Part Ten Notes / A Time of Fulfillment

Other Books by Bishop Swilley . . .

20/20 VISION

Changing Your Life
By Changing The Way You See Things

You can, in fact, change your life by changing the way that you see things. It has been theorized that there is no such thing as *reality*, there is only *perception* – a premise that can be argued, ad infinitum, by philosophers and physicists, alike. Whether or not it is actually and completely true, the fact remains that your perception of things really does determine how you think, feel and function every single day of your life. It is a fact that God is, but it is also a fact that God is to you how you see that He is. The world around you is, but that world is to you how you *see* that it is. Life is what it is, but for you, your life is how you really *see* that it is.

There are things you believe about your world that are undeniably and universally true, and there are things you believe that are only true in your own mind.

You can determine your own happiness by learning how to properly view and discern the circumstances of your past and present. By learning how to see yourself correctly, you can become the person you've always really wanted to be or, better yet, you can reveal the best "you" that you already are. You have the ability to choose an attitude and vision for each day with the same confidence and ease that you have when choosing what to have for breakfast in the morning or what clothes to wear for the day. The more you are able to see how inner sight creates daily realities, the better skilled you will become in using it to your advantage.

Free your mind, open the eyes of your heart, and prepare to change your life for the better. You **can** be happy. You **can** succeed. You **can** stop second guessing your life-choices, living in regret, or blaming others. You **can** break all the limitations of your own mind and tap into an inner power that will enable you to do things that you never thought you could do before. And you can do it all by simply choosing to change your viewpoint and perception of the things pertaining to your life. As you begin to realize personal transformation, let these words take on new meaning for you: *I once was lost, but now am found; was blind, but now I see!*

What others have to say about *20/20 VISION*

My friend, Bishop Jim Earl Swilley, has written this masterpiece that you hold in your hands and it is a sure invitation to a larger life by making that fundamental shift in your perception of reality. If you ever doubted whether God had more in store for you, this book will change your paradigm forever. Let the words of this book give you the permission you need to open the windows of your perception, change the way you view yourself and the world you live in, and watch both you and that world undergo incredible and remarkable transformation!

Mark J. Chironna, PhD
Orlando, Florida

My friend, Jim Earl Swilley, has successfully entered the marketplace of visualization and given correct spiritual understanding of a principle that literally creates success or failure, life or death, poverty or prosperity . . . Jim's book will change the lives of millions of people because he is adding vision to their sight.

Prophet Kim Clement
Prophetic Image Expressions

In a way that only he can, Bishop Jim Swilley has taken the principles of Scripture and made them practical and doable. ***20/20 VISION*** *challenges its readers to elevate their perception from being downtrodden, victimized and hopeless, to being empowered, capable and victorious.*

Bishop Eddie L. Long
Senior Pastor, New Birth Missionary Baptist Church

Bishop Swilley has done it again! His ability to provide daily insights for life is simply amazing . . . ***20/20*** *is a must read for every for believer!*

Pastor Dony McGuire
The River at Music City

This book will help you create a healthy root system by updating your underlying perceptions in all areas of your life. Through having a clear perception . . . you have the ultimate power to create your new reality and life.

Brad J. McNulty, D.C.

It's All Good

Successfully Living Your *Whole* Life Long

Pursuing peace with your ***past*** . . .
Perceiving purpose in your ***present*** . . .
Fearlessly facing your ***future*** . . .

All these themes *and more* are explored in this provocative study of the powerful implications of Romans 8:28:

> ***And we know that all things work together for good to those who love God, to those who are the called according to His purpose.***

Balancing the *secular* with the *sacred*, this candidly autobiographical and brutally honest book will make you *laugh* and make you *think*.

More importantly, it well help you begin to see how the plan for your life is unfolding every day and how God's "big picture" is revealing your destiny.

Every page contains good news and vital information about how to successfully live your ***whole* life long**. It's all here, and *it's all good!*

Keepin' It Real

Becoming a Real Person, Experiencing the Real God, in the Real World

You've never read a book quite like *Keepin' It Real!* In its pages, Bishop Swilley candidly examines an unusually wide array of subjects . . . the reality TV phenomenon . . . pop culture . . . history . . . politics . . . self-esteem . . . prosperity . . . success . . . parenting . . . multiculturalism . . . New Age philosophy . . . world religions . . . political correctness . . . racism . . . sexism . . . tolerance . . . activism . . . technology . . . addiction . . . eschatology . . . dispensationalism . . . the antichrist . . . orthodoxy . . . prayer . . . the Holy Spirit . . . destiny . . . purpose . . . vision . . . and much more . . . and addresses how they all relate to the Kingdom of God in the now!

But *Keepin' it Real* is also about *you* and how you can develop the courage and confidence to be yourself at all times and to live your *real* life without compromise. Socially relevant, thought-provoking, and theologically edgy, *Keepin' it Real* is a modern manifesto for REAL PEOPLE EXPERIENCING THE REAL GOD IN THE REAL WORLD®.

If you're ready to get *real*, get this book!

A Year In The Now!

a dynamic devotional dedicated to the daily discovery of destiny.

Would you like to . . .

. . . discover your destiny?
. . . perceive your purpose?
. . . validate your vision?
. . . reinforce your relationships?
. . . strengthen your self-esteem?
. . . overcome your obstacles?
. . . feed your faith?

You can . . . this year!
You can . . . by living in the now!
You can . . . one day at a time!

God is on your side! He is available to assist you in the pursuit of your potential as you develop the diligence to seriously search out your personal path for growth into greatness! Through seeking first His Kingdom and righteousness, you can become the person that He created you to be!

You can ONLY find God's Kingdom in the eternal "NOW" as you endeavor to experience Him in your everyday existence. Kingdom-seeking consists of a constant effort to embrace the now and a commitment to the continual conforming of your consciousness to it. This empowers and enables you to escape the mental distractions produced by living in the past or in the future, so that you can comprehend a real Christ for your current real circumstances!

A YEAR IN THE NOW! is a devotional designed to deliver a doable format for the daily development of your eternal life – to help you think creatively, beyond your familiar, time-bound comfort zones. These positive and powerful affirmations will provide the help you need to progressively put your life on the right track in realistic increments. You don't have to become overwhelmed by the tremendous task of trying to lead a "now life" in a "yesterday/tomorrow world." You can do it day by day!

This is your year to change your world! You can change your world by changing your mind! You can change your mind one day at a time!

It's time for a fresh start, and you can start right NOW!

What others have to say about *A Year In The Now!* . . .

When my dear friend, Bishop Jim Swilley sent me a copy of his new daily devotional, *A Year In The Now!*, I stopped everything I was doing and couldn't put it down . . . that is until my wife took it out of my hands and I have had to pry it back from her ever since. Jim is one of the most effective, prolific, and unique communicators I have ever met. He breaks down deep and profound truth and makes it palatable for all of us in such a practical way that just reading the principles and reciting the affirmations increases our life skills. The days are broken down into seven key principles a day, seven being the number of alignment between heaven and earth (4 being the number of earth, and three of heaven), whereby applying the seven daily truths your heart and mind are aligned with heaven's best and you are automatically brought into the kind of agreement that gets results in your life. If you want to get the "more" out of your daily life that has been promised to you in Christ I want to encourage you to get your hands on *A Year In The Now!* and make it a part of your daily spiritual discipline and focus. Oh yea, and if anyone else gets their hands on your copy in your family . . . buy another one because you won't get it back quick enough!

Dr. Mark J. Chironna
Orlando, Florida

Your devotional, *A Year in the Now!,* reads as a personal message to me. Each day I am encouraged - God is doing a new thing in the NOW! This devotional reinforces that God is working His plan in all things that affect my family and ministry. My destiny continues to unfold so that others will see my good works and glorify the Father.

Germaine Copeland
Author of Prayers That Avail Much Family Books

Deeply profound, yet 'DO-ably' practical. That's how I describe Bishop Jim Earl Swilley's *A Year In The Now!* daily devotional. Bishop Jim's 'easy to read' style of communication, combined with his witty grouping together of words that start with the same letter, define this devotional as a delightful way to delve deeper into your divine destiny as a daily discipline. Profound and practical, it's the perfect proponent to promote your personal progress.

Doug Fortune
Trumpet Call Ministry

A Year In The Now! by Bishop Jim Earl Swilley, is extraordinary and powerful, giving day by day guidance on how to be strong in the Lord through seven pearls of wisdom each day. Seven! This is God's number for completeness and fulfillment. Through A Year In The Now!, God is truly using Bishop Swilley in a mighty way to unlock the wonderful mystery of the gospel so that each of us can live abundantly, and serve God abundantly, in the now!

David Scott
United States Congressman, Georgia

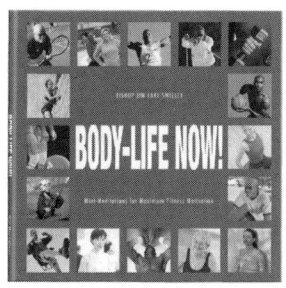

**Body-Life Now!
Mini-Meditations for Maximum Fitness Motivation**

Whether you're a serious body builder, competitive athlete, or just somebody who wants to drop a few pounds and be a little healthier than you are now, this power-devotional is for you! Inside you'll find 75 crisp little meditations on fitness, nutrition, attitude and lifestyle that will supercharge your workout and improve your outlook on your day.

You'll be doing yourself a big favor by incorporating these inspiring pages into your regular routine, *however* you choose to do so. Your spirit will be refreshed, your mind will be sharpened, and your body will thank you for the extra empowerment.

And if you're just getting *started* on the road to physical fitness, you'll find this book to be *especially* beneficial. It will serve as an easy-to-read road map for the journey designed to help you discover the new, improved *you*.

That journey can start right here . . . *and it can start right NOW!*

ABOUT THE AUTHOR

REAL PEOPLE experiencing the REAL GOD in the REAL WORLD®. This trademark of Church In The Now (CITN), founded in May, 1985 by Bishop Jim Earl Swilley, is the theme of his entire ministry. A graduate of Southeastern University in Lakeland, Florida, he began preaching on the streets of Atlanta at age 13 and, since that time, has continued to do so throughout the United States and in many countries on five continents. He served for three years as the president of a branch of New Life Bible College, is a songwriter holding membership with ASCAP, has recorded multiple music projects, and is the author of six books. In October of 1998, he was consecrated as a Bishop in the International Communion of Charismatic Churches (ICCC) and in that capacity provides oversight and covering to more than 170 churches and ministries.

Bishop Swilley is married to Debye, the Associate Pastor of CITN, and is the father of Jared, Christina, Judah and Jonah.

For more information on products or Church In The Now, please visit our website at:

www.churchinthenow.org